THE POLITICS
OF
URBAN PERSONNEL POLICY

Kennikat Press
National University Publications
Interdisciplinary Urban Series

Advisory Editor
Raymond A. Mohl

THE POLITICS
OF
URBAN PERSONNEL POLICY

REFORMERS, POLITICIANS,
AND BUREAUCRATS

WILBUR C. RICH

National University Publications
KENNIKAT PRESS // 1982
Port Washington, N.Y. // London

Manufactured in the United States of America

Published by
Kennikat Press Corp.
Port Washington, N.Y. / London

Library of Congress Cataloging in Publication Data

Rich, Wilbur C.
    The politics of urban personnel policy.

    (Interdisciplinary urban series) (National
university publications)
    Bibliography: p.
    Includes index.
    1. New York (N.Y.)–Officials and employees–
Appointment, qualifications, tenure, etc. 2. Civil
service–New York (N.Y.) 3. New York (N.Y.)–
Politics and government–1951– I. Title.
II. Series
JS1234.A4 1981   352'.0051'097471   81-5956
ISBN 0-8046-9290-4   AACR2

CONTENTS

ACKNOWLEDGMENTS

I wish to thank the following friends and colleagues who contributed their time to reading either all or part of this work in manuscript. They include Charles V. Hamilton, Harvey C. Mansfield, Sr., Phillip Monypenny, Arnold L. Steigman, Demetrios Caraley, Arthur Levine, Rondal Downing, Robert Connery, Kenneth Jackson, Helga Hilton, and Alan Z. Forman. The book owes much to their thoughtful suggestions and criticisms. None of them is responsible for whatever faults may exist in this work, all of which belong solely to the author. I would also like to thank the Council for Research in the Social Sciences (Columbia University) for its generous financial support, without which this study could not have been made. I am also grateful for the work of Regina White, who performed a monumental task of deciphering and transforming the corrected, edited pages into a finished, clearly typed manuscript.

Finally, I am indebted to my wife—Jean Russell ("Rusty")—and to my children—Rachel and Alexandra—who were tolerant and understanding throughout the entire span of this writing experience.

PREFACE

This book is about politics, values, and visions. The politics is that of the government of New York City, the nation's largest urban center, which is seeking to remain the leader in the field of personnel management. The city, which enacted the first municipal civil-service law, introduced the efficiency movement into local government, and promoted the idea of public-employee unions, is now threatened by new fiscal realities that may topple it from its preeminent position.

The values are those of the nineteenth- and twentieth-century civil service reformers' striving to impose a management view on municipal workers. The first chapter outlines the political context of the city's personnel policies and offers a theoretical framework for understanding it. To obtain an accurate picture of these ideas, it has been necessary to juxtapose reform writings and speeches with municipal records and other historical data. A systematic analysis of values promulgated in the struggle for dominance in the personnel arena has long been overdue because most students of the system have concentrated on procedural issues, such as position classification, examinations, or compensation, largely ignoring the broader political process through which personnel policies and practices are determined. This book therefore stresses the significance of the personnel process of allocating jobs, status, and income. What follows is an attempt to balance the technical and the human dimensions of personnel policy.

The vision is that of an efficient city managed by dedicated men and women. Although yet to be achieved, this dream remains alive in the city's personnel policies and politics. To analyze this vision, more than one hundred in-depth interviews were conducted. A separate random sample of more than two hundred top civil-service managers further clarified the attitudes and perceptions of employees.

New York's reputation as the most progressive city in the nation has been based on its leadership in municipal reform, its openness to new immigrants, and its willingness to provide a wide range of services to its residents. Because it provided such a vast array of services, from garbage collection to higher education, it experienced one of the worst fiscal crises in the nation's history. The fiscal crisis of 1975 came as a grim warning to the city which had attempted to continue its progressive policies in the face of declining revenues. It also serves as a reminder of how important municipal workers are to a city's operation. When garbage is left uncollected, hospital staffs reduced, and city university programs abandoned, it becomes apparent just how substantial an amount of resources and manpower is required to deliver municipal services to eight million residents.

If New York City hopes to recover and become self-sufficient again, it must further reform its personnel policies. Today the city's personnel policy has few defenders and many critics. As a result, its personnel system seems surrounded by vigilantes eager to destroy the old rules and impose new ones. For this reason, Chapter 2 analyzes the perspectives, values, and actions of several crucial interest groups: civil service reformers, politicians, political parties, public-employee unions, associations, state legislatures, mayors, and public employees themselves. Also examined are the ancillary groups that have exerted influence over personnel policy. In examining each group's behavior, the attempt has been made to treat the subject both historically and critically. At the same time, the focus is kept on intergroup dynamics, with special emphasis on how these relations influence municipal administrative policies. After nearly a century of civil service reform, the achievements of these competing groups are subject to fundamental questions, not only by public employees, but also by those in the academic and business communities and by taxpayers. For there is widespread belief that far from being an instrument of efficient government and good administrative practices, the personnel system has reinforced management flaws and legitimized the "featherbedding" penchant of municipal officials.

Any discussion of city personnel policy of necessity focuses on the power of the city's chief executive—mayoralty opportunities and limits. Recently reformers have been in the vanguard of the movement for a stronger mayoralty. The quest for control of city management starts with creating an amenable civil service system. Chapter 3 assesses the impact of reform politics on mayoral control of the personnel system.

The central role played by public-employee unions in the politics of employee relations is described in Chapter 4. This chapter examines the history of the municipal unions and of how their leadership has performed as an advocate for the membership. This group was unquestionably the ascendent group in the 1950s, 1960s, and early 1970s. The full range of rather incredible events surrounding the fiscal crisis of 1975 is beyond the scope of this book, but the impact of the crisis on personnel policy is of special interest to the current analysis. This impact may be best understood by examining the fiscal managers who became the ascendent group in city affairs. Chapter 5 reports these events and relates them to the analysis developed in previous chapters.

The effects of the New York City fiscal crisis of 1975 on the rules of competition and cooperation among groups involved in personnel politics are examined in Chapter 6. Using the metaphor of actors in a play, it seeks to describe and analyze the development of urban personnel policy in New York City in terms of drama and theatricality, and draws an analogy between the political stage and the theater in order to emphasize the dramatic nature of the process.

In the final chapter, some concluding thoughts and recommendations are proffered. These observations go beyond the New York City scene, and relate to urban personnel policy in general.

THE POLITICS
OF
URBAN PERSONNEL POLICY

Wilbur Rich is associate professor and director of the Masters in Public Administration program at Wayne State University in Detroit, Michigan. He received his Ph.D. in political science from the University of Illinois, Urbana. He is on the editorial board of *Public Administration Review, Public Productivity Review,* and has served as a consultant to civic groups, public institutions, and agencies. He is in the process of writing a textbook on urban politics.

1

INTRODUCTION

At first glance, the purpose of a city personnel system appears to be the regulation of relations between the municipality and its employees. Without such a system, the conduct of relations would lack coherence, coordination, and continuity. But this view is somewhat simplistic. A closer look at the urban personnel arena shows that it is in reality a multidimensional, dynamic political process that involves competition, negotiation, and exchange among specific interest groups. Participants are engaged in a continuous struggle for dominance, each trying to upstage the others, fighting as if in a game for stakes that include jobs, contracts, and political careers. Like characters in a melodrama their histrionics vitally affect the cost of local government and its capacity to deliver services.

The resulting political scene is one of bureaucrats and interest groups all seeking to improve or maintain their positions on the political stage, thereby creating a forum for the ambitions and claims of competing interest groups.

Many groups are participants in the drama, including public-employee unions, civil service reformers, good government groups, political parties, the office of the mayor, state legislators, and informal public employee associations. As more occasional presences, there are the press, the courts—both state and federal—and the personnel consultants. These groups and especially the office of the mayor have a significant impact on the municipal personnel system.

An examination of mayoral leadership in the history of the city of New York reveals the significance of personnel policy in the exercise of executive power. The evolution of the office of mayor has reflected the nation's anxieties about strong executives, centralized power, and one-man rule. In the city's early days the mayoralty suffered from state control and intervention in municipal administration, and in recent years it has been fragmented by a decentralization of political power. Early mayors met the first challenge by securing home rule and building strong local party organizations. The second challenge has continued to the present.

In the late 1960s, Alexander George argued that the mayors should supplement their formal authority with political skills. They should, according to Professor George, become "adept at accumulating a variety of political resources and using them to gain influence and additional resources."[1] In other words, fragmentation can be an opportunity for brokeraging, coalition building, and negotiation. Jeffrey Pressman lists seven requirements for mayoral leadership:

1. Sufficient financial and staff resources on the part of the city government.

2. City jurisdiction in social program areas, such as education, housing, redevelopment, job training, etc.

3. Mayoral jurisdiction within the city government in these policy fields

4. A salary for the mayor that would enable him to spend his full time on the job

5. Sufficient staff support for the mayor, for policy planning, speech writing, intergovernmental relations, and political work

6. Ready vehicles for publicity, such as friendly newspapers or television stations

7. Politically oriented groups, including a political party, which the mayor could mobilize to help him achieve particular goals.[2]

How have New York City's mayors met Professor Pressman's preconditions for mayoral leadership? How have they maximized their leadership potential? Through the use of individual case studies one can evaluate them on the basis of their administrative influence in personnel policy.

This mode of analysis leads to a useful classification system for mayoral strategies. First, mayors can be separated into two categories, depending upon whether they have been partisan or reform-oriented. Second, mayoral management strategies can be divided into executive-centered and department-centered. In the executive-centered strategy the mayor and his deputies seek to manage departments from City Hall. By centralizing policy, the mayor reduces the power of department heads and high-ranking civil servants.

In department-centered strategies, the mayor seeks to delegate and decentralize authority and decision-making responsibility. This approach encourages political appointees and high-ranking civil servants to work independently of City Hall. Courtesy consultation continues, but fewer clearances are needed for administrative action. Recruiting one's own staff, talking to the press, and changing department rules are encouraged under this system. For policy-making roles, the mayor often seeks professionals with national reputations and training outside the city bureaucracy. John V. Lindsay was one of the few modern-day New York City mayors to attempt to implement this approach to governing.

Regardless of the approach to policy making, the efforts are limited by the amount of time they can devote to the subject and the strength of the other interests in the personnel field. The mayoralties selected as case studies for this book demonstrate a variety of styles and results of mayoral initiatives in personnel policy making.

Reformers. Most reform organizations consider themselves public-interest groups. Jeffrey M. Berry defines a public-interest group as "one that seeks a collective good, the achievement of which will not selectively and materially benefit the membership or activists of the organization."[3] This definition applies to the civil service reform organizations discussed in this book. Individual reformers have a variety of motives for joining and supporting "good government" objectives. In any case the array of reform types makes a classification scheme necessary. Civil service reformers have therefore been divided into three groups: the genteel reformers, the academic reformers, and the fiscal managers. The genteel reformers, composed of nineteenth-century leading liberal Republicans and reform Democrats, saw the personnel system as a way of cleansing the city government of corrupting influences; they assumed an antipolitical party position and sought to influence city officials by appealing to their sense of morality. Their twentieth-century successors, the academic reformers—academics, research and personnel-management consultants—wanted to improve the civil service system by introducing business and scientific principles; they also promoted the idea of college education for city managers.

The final group discussed, the fiscal managers, came to power during the 1975 fiscal crisis. These reformers—accountants, investment specialists, and lawyers—were and are convinced that the city must have a strong fiscal and budgetary policy in order to make its revenue bonds more attractive to the investment community. The fiscal managers do not seem to have a coherent policy toward the civil service. It is this lack of policy that distinguishes these reformers from their predecessors.

Courts. It would be too glib to say that New York has a personnel system of laws, not men. Nevertheless, the fact remains that the courts have become very interested in personnel rules and procedures, in defending the standards and the constitutional rights of employees. The whole judicial system has permeated the personnel arena. Lawyers who used to practice at the margins of personnel policy (defending clients who had exhausted other administrative remedies) have become a major part of the interaction between interest groups. They see the personnel system as an arbitrary collection of rules that violate statutory and constitutional law. Judges, in turn, are more receptive to lawyers' demands for stricter adherence to rules. As a result, personnel administration has become more legalistic.

The courts have shown an interest in patronage, residency requirements, wages, union activities, and race discrimination. The rulings of the New York State courts have become major factors in the area of union negotiation and employee grievances. The state courts have been equally solicitous of employee rights and interests. They have repeatedly overruled the city's Civil Service Commission, which has had the effect of transforming simple administrative hearings into rigid judicial proceedings, complete with lawyers for both the city and the employee.

The federal courts have become the principal in the area of constitutional protection of public employees. The United States Supreme Court decision that personnel professionals worry about most is *Griggs* v. *Duke Power Company* (1971).[4] There, the court ruled that all standards for hiring and promotion must be job-related and not advantageous to any single group. Requiring a high school diploma, or a high score on an intelligence aptitude test must therefore be job-related with the burden of proof resting on the employer. Before 1971, the courts had looked for so-called evil motives when investigating cases of discrimination and stressed equal treatment as a remedy. *Griggs* redefined discrimination in terms of widespread minority deprivation, and sought to eliminate the effects of past discrimination. In so ruling the court placed severe restrictions on using examinations as a tool for personnel selection. Examinations that systematically eliminate minorities and women applicants are now illegal. This decision initiated a review of city examinations and served to increase the cost of administering written examinations.

In *McCarty* v. *Philadelphia Civil Service Commission* (1976), the Supreme Court upheld the postemployment residency requirement.[5] Under this ruling, the Civil Service Commission could issue a regulation requiring that all New York City employees live in the city. The public-employee unions, however, have so far been able to block passage of such a requirement; they have been supported by the state courts and state legislature. Since the ruling, Mayors Abraham Beame and Edward Koch have supported residency laws but have failed to convince the state legislature in Albany, whose consent is required for any city action, to pass them. The estimate is that about 20 percent of the city work force (40,000) now live outside the city. Of these, 12,000 are policemen (one-third of the force), 36 percent are firemen, 11 percent sanitationmen, and 10 percent Board of Education personnel.[6]

In 1976 the Supreme Court ruled in *Abood* v. *Detroit Board of Education* that a union which is the exclusive bargaining agent for city workers can collect the functional equivalent of dues (service charges) from nonunion employees to cover services provided by the union.[7] The service fee, however, cannot be used for political activity outside of collective bargaining. This ruling legalized the role of the agency shop in public employment. The willingness to use a private-sector model again demonstrates the narrowness of the court's vision with respect to the special nature of public employment. In effect, the court is forcing the question of whether unions are political organizations. The lower courts will have to decide which are political and which are collective-bargaining activities. This ruling allowed New York unions to begin the collection of fees from nonunion members.

Political Parties. Of the various active forces in the political arena (including interest groups), the political parties have been the most affected by changes in the personnel system. The urban personnel system historically was a reaction against intraparty disputes, single-party domination, corruption, and patronage. Most research on city personnel neglects the role of political parties, or attempts to portray their role in a negative light. The parties, however, played a central role in the functioning of personnel administration; they are indispensable to democratic government and may well continue to influence urban personnel policy.

With this in mind, several questions emerge regarding the importance of political parties to the personnel system. What can be done to retain their counsel in city decision making? Is there some way to reconcile nonpartisan administration with demands for patronage? What type of patronage should be removed totally from party control? How can city administrators use the local party linkages between state and national governments to enhance the effectiveness of city agencies? Should public employees be restricted from participating in party activities? Finally, What have been the consequences of removing parties from city administration?

Answers to such questions require an analysis into the actual role played by parties in the making of personnel policy. E. E. Schattschneider has observed:

In effect . . . the parties frame the question and define the issue. In doing this they go a long way toward determining what the answer will be.[8]

As a part of their organizing and staffing responsibility, parties have been primarily concerned with getting the so-called right people into government. Partisans usually define right people as those who "identify with party goals and ideology." In the nineteenth century, the parties were an important—but not absolute—determinant in the recruitment of public employees. The advent of civil service reform saw this role diminish as more groups asserted responsibility for this task. Many people, however, still consider political parties a viable channel through which to attain employment in government.

Political parties, as mobilizing organizations, regard civil service reform as a threat to their sources of influence in city affairs. Party leaders have seen their patronage and political control over elected officials reduced. Because they no longer provide welfare services and job referrals, it has become extremely difficult for the parties to compete with other interest groups for the loyalty of public employees. Mayors since Thomas Gilroy (1893-1894) have attempted to gain more control over the bureaucracy through dilution of the rigid competitive-examination system, reorganization, and decentralization. On the whole, the mayors' record in civil service reform has been mixed. Despite the support of reformers and urban-management experts, mayors have yet to develop an executive-centered form of government.

Even though the parties in New York City are no longer the single political kingmakers, candidates still must appeal to the middle-class constituency within political clubs if they expect to be elected. Thus, they will stress merit recruitment to satisfy educated voters, and blast landlords to appease tenant groups; in appealing to unions, candidates may oppose job quotas for minorities, and criticize city management or the employment of part-time workers.

The political party provides a forum for vocalizing such views. In performing this brokerage role, it can be openly ideological and uncompromising—something other interest groups can ill afford.

Another function of political parties is to educate bureaucrats about the needs of city residents. Bureaucrats are often insensitive to the changing demographic patterns in urban areas, and unaware that they are representatives of the people. In New York, this takes the form of reform procedures in city departments, with academics and technocrats "force-feeding" new policies. The Lindsay reforms are typical in this sense. Mayor Lindsay came to power as a liberal Republican, bringing with him a group of zealous young men intent upon reforming city administration.

Parties contribute to personnel policy making via the legislative and executive processes by helping to elect councilmen, state legislators, and mayors. In the past, parties could exact obligations from these officials. Today this is not so widespread, although party support is still needed for some city department commissionerships.

In New York the absence of a strong party system has promoted a personalized network of relationships. Political clubs provide office-holders with an opportunity to meet with potential rivals. Here social interaction is critical to individual as well as to collective advancement. Reformist clubs have been staunch supporters of the merit system of recruitment. Other clubs have advocated a "mixed" system; that is, a combination of merit and patronage. Both types of clubs are opposed to bureaucratic red tape.

Public-Employee Unions. Public-employee unions have viewed New York City workers as underpaid and overworked, and at the same time as a potentially powerful political force. They have organized the civil servants into a group that resembles the private sector's counterpart: trade and craft unions. The municipal unions' interest in the personnel system and civil service reform is primarily in the areas of wages, pensions, job security, and employee rights. With the advent of the 1975 fiscal crisis, the public-employee pension funds have become a critical part of the city's borrowing capacity. As a result, unions have increased their political power and decreased investment flexibility; that is to say, the managers of union pension funds are not free to invest in stocks or bonds that have greater yields and stronger ratings, but politically the unions have increased their power because they have convinced the new fiscal managers that they should play a larger role in fiscal and personnel decisions.

State Legislature. Throughout the years the state legislature has continued to play a major role in municipal personnel policy making. State approval is still needed for every major change in city civil service rules. Since the inception of the civil service, the New York State Civil Service Commission has investigated abuses of the state civil service laws that apply to municipalities. The state legislature has continually refused to pass municipal residency laws or to make legal exceptions for some city employees. Many local groups, especially unions, have a sympathetic audience in the state legislature in regard to municipal personnel issues.

Public Employees. Finally, the public employees themselves have played a role in personnel decisions. Workers have resisted rule changes, voted down contract recommendations of union leaders, and established informal organizations for protection from arbitrary management intervention. In so doing, they have created yet another veto point along the line of municipal personnel decisions.

GROUP POLITICS AND CLASS MOBILITY

In this book personnel politics and management are examined from both the historical and sociological viewpoint in an attempt to link past events with present conditions. In depicting the personnel arena as a theater of group competition for jobs, status, and dominance, Karl Mannheim's typology of class mobility seems appropriate. Mannheim identified four types of classes: ascendent, declining, threatened, and newly conscious.

The ascendent class is the emerging middle class whose power and status are on the rise. The declining class (the old regime) is composed of those groups whose control over events is coming to an end. The threatened class comprises the target group, and is a rival of the ascendent groups. The former's interests are immediately affected by the proposals and actions of the latter. The newly conscious class is formed by changes in the array of groups or economic conditions. New groups may arise as a reaction to the excesses of ascendent and threatened groups.

The present study traces the replacement of the mercantile capitalists— that is, of the shipping and landowning gentry (the declining class)— in public affairs. This transition period saw a huge increase in population, the growth of political machines, and the emergence of New York City as the leading industrial metropolis in the nation. The resulting change in leadership in economic affairs had serious implications for the evolution of city government and personnel transactions. The early civil service reformers (the genteel reformers), the supplicants of the new capitalists, repudiated Tammany Hall's control of government, and practically eliminated its sources of patronage. These reformers were also the promoters of meritocracy. They believed that merit principles would solve most, if not all, of the problems of municipal government. Mannheim has described the utopian ideology as a part of the psychological makeup of ascendent classes:

The utopia of the ascendent bourgeoise was the idea of "freedom." It was in part a real utopia, i.e., it contained elements oriented towards the realization of a new social order which were instrumental in disintegrating the previously existing order and which, after their realization, did in part become translated into reality. Freedom in the sense of bursting asunder the bonds of the static, guild, and caste order, in the sense of freedom and freedom of the unhampered development of the personality became to a large extent, or at least to a greater extent than in the preceding status-bound, feudal society, a realizable possibility.[9]

In addition to Mannheim's four types of classes, there exists another group, which consists of an artificially aggregated category of individuals. This group is composed of individuals lumped together by institutions merely for identification. The members do not regard themselves as a collective entity; they share attributes, titles, and values, but they are neither organized nor prepared to articulate their notion of utopia; i.e., a plan for the future. Without a vision of the future, they tend to be present-oriented, conservative, and passive. The mini-case study presented in Chapter 6 suggests that managers belong to this category of artificially aggregated individuals. Civil service managers have been the least able to defend themselves against the challenge and aggression of other groups.

The personnel arena allows all these groups to assert their particular notions of a perfect personnel system. The polemic postures assumed by individual groups or their spokesmen must be understood in terms of their own self-interest. The personnel arena has no room for autonomous or disinterested individuals or groups. Even the reform journalists and writers who produced the bulk of the literature on personnel history did so in response to the needs of their group—the middle class—in order to defend its privileges or advantages over other groups.

As a theater of ascendent groups and ambitious mayors, the history of the city's civil service provides quite an informative account of the relative strengths and weaknesses of the various groups and individuals. This checkered history reminds us that electoral victory is ephemeral and that political power is as delicate as it is addictive. The addiction to power led some reformers to form a working relationship with their nemesis—Tammany Hall. Reformers also discovered that getting the audience's attention had to be followed by providing them with a good show. When they failed to do so, their candidates were rejected. Great leaps forward in civil service recruitment were easily reversed by partisan mayors; reform charters were replaced by more flexible ones.

The numerous revisions of the city charter all failed to place the mayor foursquare on the top of the bureaucracy. Indeed, many revisions have been myopic in terms of the long-range management needs of the office. The various combinations of power-sharing involving the mayor, borough presidents, and the Board of Estimate were designed to gain more control over the management of city government. The mayor can set priorities by intense and conscientious dramaturgy, but because his office is structurally out of touch with the day-to-day activities of the bureaucracy and the conflicting demands of the various audiences, he cannot follow through on many administrative promises.

The partisan bureaucracy allowed the party to manage the system effectively but not efficiently. Unfortunately, the party-sponsored mayors were not paragons of a strong and independent executive. The party controlled them as it did the bureaucratic recruitment. Had strong leaders of Tammany, such as William M. Tweed or Richard Croker become mayor, the history of mayoral power might well have been different. At least there would have been a convergence of party and government leadership.

Both the genteel reformers and their successors, the academic reformers, were able to undermine the role of the party in civil service affairs. They were able to identify themselves as "good government" and characterize their opponents' organizations as citadels of corruption and prodigality. The combination of this history, these interests, and the requirements of policy implementation makes New York a good laboratory for examining the group dynamics of personnel administration.

NEW YORK CITY AS A CASE STUDY

New York City provides a valuable case study for analyzing municipal personnel policy. Aside from developing the first city civil service system, it has always been a leader in municipal reform. In addition to its size, its history, and its population diversity, it has also the largest urban bureaucracy. In 1975 it had more than 300,000 employees, a number bigger than the total population of most moderate-sized American cities, and it has a budget larger than the budget of India. The municipal hospital system alone has more people in it than the governments of most underdeveloped nations. New York is the only city in the nation with its own higher-education system. As the center of finance, communications, and the arts, its importance cannot be challenged. It is not surprising that its politics are among the most exciting in the nation.

Present-day personnel politics in New York City are crowded with diverse, fiercely competing groups and individuals seeking to make economic claims or political reputations. The first and most obvious actors are the mayor and his close advisers. The mayor of New York, like his counterpart in most urban communities, operates within an *economy of patronage.* The mayor has always had to share power in the allocation of municipal patronage. As the present volume aims to make clear, the evolution of the office has been accompanied by the mayor's effort to gain more control over personnel decisions. The creations of the office of budget director and the office of personnel director were attempts to give the mayor added leverage in the personnel arena. Nevertheless, mayors have failed to dominate the personnel arena because the power of the executive office has always been open to dilution by the extant ascendent group, whose chief weapon is charter revision.

The evolution of the Civil Service Commission in the nineteenth and early twentieth centuries provides an example of reform at the expense of the mayor and other elected officials. The framer of the municipal Civil Service Commission demanded and received political insulation from partisan politics. With the blessings of reform Democrats and liberal Republicans in the state legislature, the commission supplanted the parties' monopoly over recruitment, which until then had been enjoyed by Tammany Hall. It was not until the Mitchel (1914–1917) and LaGuardia (1934–1945) administrations that mayors attempted to change personnel policy through commission appointments. The gains achieved by these reform mayors were quickly abandoned by their immediate successors, John Hylan and William O'Dwyer respectively.

As reformers grew less interested in serving as civil service commissioners, mayors began to use the offices of the commission as patronage plums. These part-time positions were quietly handed out to campaign supporters of the mayor. The present-day commission, lacking the prestige and the reform constituency of its nineteenth century predecessors, serves as a sounding board for the municipal personnel director and as an appeal board for employee grievances. It no longer performs a quasi-executive function. Since the 1950s the actual duties of personnel management, such as rule making, appeals classification, and examinations, have been performed by the city's new Department of Personnel.

The Department of Personnel has had a shaky history. In 1951, the Civil Service Reform Association lamented that the city budget director was "the real personnel administrator of the city." The association's warning that the Civil Service Commission was becoming a pliant scapegoat may have been an exaggeration, but historical evidence suggests that the expansion of the budget director's duties (e.g., review of agency personnel requests) has been at the expense of the personnel director. The record also suggests that personnel policy has been too amenable to the policies and personality of the personnel director.

Under the talented leadership of Joseph Schechter (1954–1959) and

Sol Hoberman (1966–1970), the office was regarded as a model for the nation, but its preeminence in the local personnel arena has been eclipsed by the Office of Municipal Labor Relations (OMLR). This office, created by John V. Lindsay as the negotiating unit of the mayor, now dictates employee decisions to the personnel department. The Department of Personnel, which was hailed in the 1950s as bringing professionalism to municipal personnel administration, has now been reduced to an assemblage of clerks. The OMLR with a staff of fifty-seven persons and a budget of more than a million dollars oversees the implementation of personnel guidelines and conducts collective bargaining.

The Office of Collective Bargaining (OCB) describes itself as analogous to the National Labor Relations Board or the state's Public Employee Relation Board (PERB) in its function; it certifies collective-bargaining representatives, promulgates procedures, creates mediation and impasse panels, and arbitrates labor disputes and disagreements between the city and its workers.

The picture emerging from these competing bureaucracies is one of duplication and rivalry, confused even further by the courts, the state legislature, and the federal government. The courts have ruled on questions ranging from the power of the Civil Service Commission to make rules and hear appeals to the fine print in a labor contract. The state legislature has always encroached upon the city's prerogatives in personnel matters, simply because the distribution of local patronage affects state politics. To this day the state still retains the power to take over the Civil Service Commission, investigate personnel practices, and make laws binding on city workers.

This book does not offer any normative judgments about the groups competing in the public personnel arena; nor does it embrace as clearly preferable any of the values presented by them. In order to capture the specific perspective of each group, the study employs the concept of politics as theater, a device that delineates the interesting variety of tactics and strategies used by these groups. To regard personnel politics as a theater of ascendent groups is not to deny the importance of traditional analysis of city management; instead the purpose of the book is to enable us better to understand the results of traditional analysis while at the same time permitting an enlarged perspective yielding new insights.

2

GENTEEL REFORMERS
AND THE POLITICAL MACHINES

The accepted historical characterization of Tammany Hall's political control over New York City's municipal workers as malevolent, corrupt, and inept is on the whole an inaccurate one. The weight of evidence suggests that the reformers exaggerated the misdeeds of Tammany politicians and overstated the reform contribution in the development of the civil service system. In order to appreciate the interaction between the reformers and Tammany, one must return to the genesis of the relationship. Without such perspective, any view of the present personnel system would be one-dimensional. In this chapter, therefore, the emergence of Tammany as the leading interest group in the personnel arena, and the events that led to civil service reform are to be reviewed.

In many ways, the struggle for control of the public-employment arena started in the eighteenth century. New York, or the Village of Manhattan as it was then called, was the flagship of the mercantile nation. It had shipbuilders, manpower, and a natural port. Yet it could hardly have been considered a gem of the British Empire, for it was a large congested village with, among other deficiencies, unpaved streets and unpaid firemen. Under the colonial system, the village never developed a municipal government in the sense that the term is understood today.

The Montgomerie Charter of 1777 was a limited one, and the many administrative powers remained in the hands of state officials. The city administration was shared by the state government and locally elected aldermen. The Council of Appointment, a form of state board of directors consisting of the governor and a senator elected by the state assembly from each of New York State's four districts, appointed the city's mayor, commissioners of health, surrogates, recorder, common clerk, police justices, sheriff, and district attorney.[1]

The Common Council, which combined both legislative and executive functions, consisted of elected aldermen, assistant aldermen, the recorder, and the mayor. Although the mayor presided over council meetings, he was by no means the chief executive officer. The mayor, under this charter, was a judicial officer, the presiding justice of the Mayor's Court and the Court of General Sessions, and served as a member of the Court of Oyer and Terminer. In other words, the mayor was a judicial officer. The notion that the mayor is an executive and administrative officer was conceived in the second quarter of the nineteenth century.[2]

Although the mayor shared administrative and executive responsibility with the Common Council, he was also charged with some ceremonial and housekeeping functions, which allowed him to distribute patronage. He appointed the inspectors of hay, a deputy bailiff, scavengers, public porters, packers, and cullers. In 1800, there were 40 deputy marshals and 1,050 cartmen, all of whom were appointed by the mayor.[3] Any leverage the mayor had came from the patronage he was able to dispense, not from the power of his office.

Throughout the early part of the nineteenth century, the Common Council wielded more power than the mayor in Manhattan affairs. The control of personnel administration and thus of patronage was in the hands of the council. The actual supervision of public services was delegated, however, to the standing committees of the council, including control over patronage (i.e., appointing chief officers, distributing jobs to individuals and making vendor contracts). By 1804, there were eight standing committees in charge of the day-to-day administrative services.

In many respects the administrative structure resembles the modern version of the commission form of municipal government, and in fact a closer examination reveals that the council had many of the same problems as the commission form of government. These problems, then and now, stem from the imbalance between legislative and executive functions. A government by committee is a government with too many decision makers and too few decision implementers. Professor Winter has identified two glaring defects in this sort of administration: the absence of clear-cut executive authority, and amateur administration. He adds:

Since all authority was concentrated in the council, it would seem, at first glance, that the maximum of concentrated authority was achieved by commission government. This was not, however, the case. Although the council as a body could, and did, act in a legislative and executive capacity, it could not by itself administer policy. Policy administration became divided and isolated into many islands of responsibility.

If internal dissension does develop, the results are just as striking. A permanent majority opposed to a permanent minority splits the city's administration wide open. Where departments were once uncoordinated, but at least neutral toward each other, now they are active enemies. Here is separation of powers in its most virulent form. But instead of the classic separation—legislative, executive, and judicial—this is separation in the administration itself. Here is a perfect situation for buck-passing. The majority will insist that malfunctioning of the minority department is causing the failure of the city's administration; the minority will insist, with equal justification, that the majority has hamstrung the minority departments.[4]

This type of administration may have been adequate for the simple housekeeping functions of a small village, but as the population increased, so did the services provided by the government. The rapid increases in population, which from 1810 to 1830 rose from 96,373 to 202,589,[5] forced the state to reconsider its policy of a weak executive. In 1830, charter revision granted the mayor veto power over council decisions. This established a check-and-balance mechanism that ended the subordination of the mayor to department heads.

Interest Groups and Municipal Expansion. During this early period of the city's history, a coalition of landed gentry or aristocracy and mercantile interests (i.e., shipping and commerce) dominated public affairs. This coalition saw no need to enlarge the city government, advocate home rule, or increase the power of the mayor. Restricting the government to light housekeeping, and the mayor to ceremonial and judicial duties, slowed the growth of powerful political figures and political organizations. Aside from a relatively expensive program of public relief, the government provided few social services to city residents; the needy relied on charity and mutual (and ethnic) benevolent societies. Private organizations took care of the poor, and the Free School Society educated indigent children.[6] The city had a volunteer fire department and a small police force.[7] When the business boom burst in 1837 with the onset of the nation's first major depression, the need for a reorganization of municipal government and the expansion of human services became apparent.[8] It had also become clear to those with business interests that they could no longer safely ignore Tammany Hall's political potential. With the advent of an elected mayor in 1824, there had emerged a working relationship between the small Tammany Society and the dominant financial interests. Tammany supported political candidates from the mercantile community in municipal elections and in turn received a free hand in local patronage. The mercantile influence is exemplified by the backgrounds of the nineteenth-century mayors and their occupations from 1810 to 1901: of the thirty-eight mayors appointed or elected during this period, nineteen were merchants, food manufacturers, or small businessmen.[9]

During this period the onetime village had been transformed into an overcrowded small city. The city muddled through with a weak mayor, a small work force, and no planning staff. Reformers understood the new problems of the city but feared any expansion of the municipal work force. They believed that a larger work force would increase the patronage of elected mayors. With such an expansion, Tammany Hall could dominate city politics.

By the early 1840s, Tammany was able to achieve control over some city jobs. As the government grew, so did the influence of Tammany Hall. By the mid-1840s the demand for municipal jobs exceeded the supply. Tammany was faced with two choices. It could push for more autonomous department heads, who could hire and fire, or it could back a strong executive form of government—the latter would allow the party to distribute patronage jobs from the top. With the election of William F. Havemeyer in 1844, the Tammany Democrats received the worst of both worlds: a weak mayor and further decentralization of patronage.

Mayor Havemeyer, a sugar refiner, began a personal crusade for a new charter that would mandate elected department heads. Yet though the Havemeyer proposal did remove the Common Council from day-to-day administration of city departments, it did not strengthen the executive power of the mayor. The charter revisions of 1849 gave elected department heads the power to nominate their own superintendent of bureaus. The charter also required the departments to produce an annual report.

Until this time, city records were not systematically maintained. The annual reports, however, did not solve the political-party patronage problem. Tammany and the competing parties wanted a mayoralty free of shared power, with total control over patronage. In 1855, Tammany mayor Fernando Wood complained bitterly about the lack of mayoral authority in administering the city:

Amendments to the charter of 1830 have, one after another, been adopted at Albany, until now we are administering the government by portions of *six different charters, which create nine executive departments, having undefined, doubtful, and conflicting powers,* with heads elected by the people, *each assuming to be sovereign, and independent of the others, of the Mayor, or of any other authority;* and beyond the reach of any, except that of impeachment by the Common Council, which never has been, and probably never will be exercised.[10]

Mayor Wood's pleas were not supported by the pre-Civil War reformers. These reformers were convinced—as was James Madison, one of the framers of the United States Constitution—that divided powers prevent a monopoly of power by one person. Many of the reformers were white Anglo-Saxon Protestant (WASP) Republicans and regarded most Democrats as incompetent spoilsmen ready to pad the city's payrolls with immigrants. Others believed that government was at its most efficient when it had the least to do. The Civil War changed this view, and made the growth of local government inevitable. The end of the war set the stage for Tammany's drive for the first strong, executive-dominated government in the city's history.

The Tweed Charter and Personnel Administration. In 1870 William M. Tweed allegedly paid $100,000 in bribes to state legislators to secure a new charter that gave the mayor control over city departments. The new charter was a major victory for Tammany Hall, for it established home rule on solid ground and strengthened the office of the mayor. For the first time, the mayor of New York City was empowered to appoint department heads without state approval. The new charter also gave the Tweed organization considerable authority to recruit personnel without clearing appointments with upstate politicians. The centralization of authority obviated personal entrepreneurship, which Seymour Mandelbaum has regarded as critical to decision making before 1870. He has observed:

In a society of independent, individual decision-makers, the mechanisms of the marketplace, which gave every commodity and every man a price, dominated society. Individual decisions were cumulated in the market, resources were allocated, the quality of life determined. The market's . . . criterion for choice [was] : "How much will you pay?" and "How much do you want?" There appeared to be no other mechanism capable of making decisions on a more complex set of criteria. The alternative to decentralized market decision-making, men of good spirit believed, was an ignorant autocracy. Even humane acts of charity were suspect because they ignored the criteria of the marketplace. They threatened the insistence on the individual responsibility in a society which could not collectively solve its problems. Individuals had to be forced into the marketplace, where problems could be solved.[11]

Historians have perpetuated the myth that with the new charter Boss Tweed gained absolute control of patronage in the city. Historians Mandelbaum and Leo Hershkowitz have rejected this thesis. Mandelbaum attributes Tweed's behavior as a rational response to an unstable marketplace. "Tweed's purchases of political support and his thievery were simply the ultimate extension of the dominance of the dollar vote."[12] Hershkowitz views Tweed's behavior in very different terms. According to his view, "even the dreaded 'Tammany Tiger' was a paper one. Certainly in Tweed's day Tammany did not dominate New York politics. Perhaps it never did."[13]

Hershkowitz's research suggests that Tweed was a victim of irresponsible journalism, opponents of mass democracy, and rival politicians. Hershkowitz may not have succeeded in debunking all the myths about Tweed, but his data support the current thesis, i.e., that Tweed's performance was in no way unique for city officials in the nineteenth century, nor did it represent an aberration from the norm. Aside from the unsubstantiated claims of the reformers, there is no substantive evidence that Tweed's personnel policies were nefarious, inefficient, or excessively self-serving.

There is little evidence that Boss Tweed had any philosophy of administration. In his time, face-to-face relationships were extremely important, as were the ties to ethnic groups and social classes. Workers were valued because of their loyalty, rather than for their ability to perform specific tasks. Administrative decisions—which today would be guided by considerations of efficiency, cost-benefit analysis, and the law—were in Tweed's day influenced much more by norms of reciprocity, ethnic considerations, and political advantages.

The evidence suggests that in order to lead the Democratic party or to conduct its business with government, Tweed was forced to rely on incentives to induce compliance. Thus city workers were given good wages; politicians, good status; state legislators, bribes. As elected leader of the Tammany Society, Boss Tweed was subject to strict accountability to his political party and the city. He had to deliver to both constituencies. The public expected Tammany to distribute patronage consistent with its sources of support. Politicians are not known for being magnanimous toward their opponents in the distribution of the spoils of victory. The infamous George Washington Plunkett stated in crude form the practice followed by reformers and Tammany alike:

When the people elected Tammany, they knew just what they were doin'. We didn't put up any false pretenses. We didn't go in for humbug civil service and all that rot. We stood as we have always stood, for rewardin' the men that won the victory. They call that the spoils system. All right; Tammany is for the spoils system, and when we go in we fire every anti-Tammany man from office that can be fired under the law. It's an elastic sort of law and you can bet it will be stretched to the limit.[14]

Although Plunkett may have overstated the zeal for change in the administration, his comments suggest that the public and the city workers understood the obligations involved in civil service employment. In six of eight post-Civil War mayoralty elections, New York City's civil servants supported Tammany Hall mayors. Reform administrations were rarely reelected even after civil service reform. Why then did the public and the city workers prefer Tammany? An attempt to answer this important question follows.

Working in a Tammany Administration. Under Tweed, there were few written rules and regulations governing city workers. Transactions between the various city departments and the public were conducted without records, files, or transcripts. Apart from the traditions and customs that evolved from each department, the bureaucrats had few guidelines to follow. Written competitive examinations for city employees were not introduced until 1882. Until then, very few jobs required a high degree of literacy; nepotism and lateral entrance into positions were very common in most departments. There was no separation of job and incumbency. People were assigned to jobs according to their experience. Usually a person could rely on receiving his job preference, as long as the needs of the political machine were met.[15]

Contrary to reformer propaganda, illiterates were rarely assigned clerical duties, nor were the well-educated given a street broom. Nevertheless, educated workers, like others, had to be sponsored by a party official to get a permanent position. If one happened to be the protégé of a leading party figure, one's chances of upward mobility within a department increased. A partisan bureaucracy did not stress job security because to use writer Abby H. Ware's phrase, it was not "within the gift of city."[16] There were no pension plans, strong employee associations, nor unions in existence. The use of temporary day laborers by Tammany was an essential and deliberate employment strategy, enabling the party to keep its visibility high in immigrant communities, and by using day laborers, the organization did not have to pay such fringe benefits as pensions and injury compensation.

There was as much job security in a partisan bureaucracy as an election allowed. Nobody's job was safe if he failed to pull his share of the load during the election. Even support for a boss eroded if his part of the organization suffered repeated defeats. On an individual level, the appointed official had no protection against arbitrary dismissal. But this did not mean that there was a high turnover rate, for a prudent public servant would often cultivate influential sponsors when the party was in power, and make himself scarce when it was not. Since the Democrats usually dominated the elections, an employee needed only to belong to the right faction of the party to keep his job. The usual grounds for dismissal of a partisan bureaucrat were attributable to his failure to vote for the party, his refusal to assist local party officials in mobilizing voters, or his failure to pay political assessments. The partisan bureaucrat had no formal grievance procedure to which to appeal if he were fired or transferred. There was no formal salary scale; a person was paid as much as he was thought worth to the department and the party. This situation led to kickbacks, sinecures, and "no-show" jobs.

With machinations such as these, the major source of income for the party was the political assessment or tax. Naturally, partisan bureaucrats resented these assessments, so reformers played on their resentment in order to enlist their support. As Dorman Eaton has observed:

The claim that political assessments are voluntarily paid by officials is contradicted by all experience and by the very methods of their collection. The officers are singled out, as a class, and are separately approached and threatened. The language of the demands is not only for a specific sum or percent never addressed to others, but is made in such peremptory language any private citizen would resent. The fear that a removal will follow a refusal or omission to pay—that is the exercise of the liberty which every private citizen asserts for himself—is universal, and it is warranted by long usage.[17]

The party repeatedly justified these assessments as necessary for organization and election expenses. It is not clear whether the fee was a graduated or regressive levy. The growing resentment of the assessment and the lack of a fair compensation system may have encouraged some street-level bureaucrats to engage in petty bribe taking. At times, this may have alienated the public. There was little relationship then, as now, between a person's level of compensation and his willingness to ask for or accept a bribe.

In summary, the Tammany-controlled departments were labor-incentive organizations, which had the flexibility to respond to an unstable marketplace. Because they provided few direct social services—welfare and casework were under the domain of the party—city departments could afford to operate in an ad hoc manner.

In the early 1880s, businessmen no longer needed the Tammany machine to facilitate their relationship with the public. They had made their fortune during the Civil War and now sought a new social image. Some backed their reform-oriented colleagues, lawyers, and clergymen, who wanted to undercut the power of Tammany and establish a non-partisan bureaucracy. The majority did not publicly identify with the civil service reformers, but some privately contributed to reform organizations. The primary strategy of this movement was to weaken Tammany's grasp on the working class by exposing crimes committed by Tammany officeholders. The reformers also convinced businessmen who were their colleagues, supporters, and clients, that a British-style civil service system would serve as a buffer against a Tammany-organized and -educated middle class, that it was necessary to depoliticize the emerging middle class.

The vision of future Tammany chieftains with college degrees loomed as a new threat on the urban scene. The genteel reformers sought to coopt the politics of the middle class by supporting the infant nonpolitical organizations, mutual benefit societies, and professional associations. Their idea was to have middle-class professionals concentrate their energies on developing professional values and standards. The concept of the professional, or of one whose basic loyalty is to a specific set of ethics and rules, emerged as the credo of new associations of the late nineteenth century. Reformers found willing supporters in the young professional organizations to whom they promised job security and organizational recognition. Professional association members joined the civil service movement and became some of its most enthusiastic workers. After the enactment of the state's civil service laws, the reformers supported the professional associations' quest for recognition through licensing and registration. The professional associations' ethics and standards were later incorporated into state and city licensing and registry laws.

The civil service reform movement became the vanguard of an effort to make government service a profession without immersion in partisan politics. The strength behind Tammany Hall lay in petty patronage and in the dispensing of temporary work. In order to undermine Tammany's base of support, a new class of employees and positions had to be institutionalized in the city government. Reformers decided on a strategy that imposed recruitment restrictions on new city workers and promoted the idea of upward social mobility in government service. The new middle class, perhaps in its efforts to strip itself of its working-class background or its conversion to civil service doctrine, embraced the civil service movement. Its members became crusaders for business principles, efficiency, and nonpartisan government.[18]

Unlike their British counterparts, the American reformers were not interested in developing a higher civil service to control government administration. They wanted a depoliticized bureaucracy to replace party influence and unaccountability in government. Although members of the domestic civil service would identify with the upper class they would be recruited from second-generation, immigrant, high-school graduates. The institutions of the merit system and strict business and accounting methods helped to develop a permanent middle-management strata with an apolitical posture. Other improvements included the banning of political assessments (i.e., regular kickbacks of a certain percentage of one's salary to one's political party) and the increased status of the civil service through the establishment of competitive examinations for jobs. In order to create this new class of workers, the reformers had to discredit and replace Tammany.

REFORMERS AND THE MERIT PRINCIPLE

Tammany had a reputation for championing the notion of "to the victors belong the spoils." In this case the spoils were the hearts and minds of the electorate; the victors, whichever of the contestants best shaped the debate. The reformers proved to be the better debaters; they were able to persuade the public that their side of the issue was right. Tammany was simply unable to defend its record or develop a credible argument against the so-called merit principle.

The term "merit principle" was used to legitimate the existing distribution of well-paying and skill-oriented civil service positions. By adding educational requirements or literacy to job qualifications, these reformers virtually eliminated the uneducated as competitors. The working class acquiesced to these new literacy requirements. Their acceptance gave the advantage to job applicants with schooling and helped to institutionalize middle-class preeminence in city departments.

Adequate assessment of the basis of power must therefore include an examination of political rhetoric and activities of both the proponents and opponents of the merit principle. To accomplish this, the theoretical framework of the historical data must be analyzed. Also, in order to reveal a direct relationship, the speeches and writings of reform politicians must be examined in the light of the leading social philosophies of the nineteenth and twentieth centuries. In making this important linkage, the various usages of the term *merit* will be investigated. In this case the term merit was characterized as a Darwinist, moral, or political imperative, the description of merit being dependent upon the audience and the speaker's objective.

Merit as a Struggle Among Men. The merit principle, especially where its competitive component is emphasized, is a form of social Darwinism, the principles of which deny the positive benefits of the political party's brokerage or regulatory functions. Adherents of this point of view believe that welfare-oriented party officials tend to pander to the weak, incompetent, and indolent in exchange for their votes. They also believe that individual liberty is constrained by the requirements of party and union membership. The individual is not free to exhibit his wares in competition with others for the goods of life.

Social Darwinism, in positing a kind of laissez-faire ideology, also advocates a limited government. Although many civil service reformers would not call themselves social Darwinists outright, their writings indeed support these ideas.[19] The genteel reformers argued that an open civil-service recruitment system would serve the interest of good government because it would eliminate the obviously unfit and incompetent; in other words, good competition yields good workers. Such views may be reduced to three basic propositions:

1. The idea that politics is an open arena where men seek to prove themselves. This is the natural order of things and bureaucrats, like others, have the right to compete.

2. Only the "best men" can produce efficient administration.

3. The public interest is served if the best men govern.

The proponents of these views also argue that merit is the equitable and unbiased method of choosing between applicant individuals and groups. The assumption is made that the rules of the game are defined by merit; as a result the contest is one of survival of the fittest. The best people will emerge from such competition. It is wrong and unnatural for political parties or officials to give the weak an artificial advantage. The winners in such a contest have the first claim on the rewards offered by society. The proponents of this kind of merit system ignore, however, the existing socioeconomic inequities and structural obstacles that prevent a true competition.

Many groups and individuals (e.g., the non-English speaking and the illiterate) start under a severe handicap. Because they cannot compete equally with others, the merit system preserves an inequality of opportunity. In other words, the most educated and socially acceptable person will always have an advantage in an open system. Assuming that all the starting places are aligned does not necessarily make for a fair race. In any case, the early reformers were able to institutionalize an open and vertical recruitment system in the city of New York. They had less success in selling the idea of the merit system.

The ideology behind the development of a merit system and its concomitant vertical promotion principle was initially articulated by the founders of the New York City Civil Service Commission and its first commissioners, Everett Wheeler and Edwin Godkin. Wheeler summarized the goals of such a system as follows:

What we desire to accomplish is this: Every American father should be able, in considering the occupation that he will select for his son: every American youth, in considering the calling that he will select for himself, should be able to consider as one of these the civil service of his country. He should be able to feel that, if he applies for admission to it, diligence and patient application in the free school will tell. He should be able to feel that, however humble his parentage or his previous station, his country gives to him an opportunity equal to that she gives to those who in other respects have been more favored. He should be able to feel that, if he is admitted to this service, his country will not be unfaithful to him so long as he is faithful to her. If he shows fitness, he will be retained. If he shows special skill and diligence, he will be promoted.[20]

These words echoed the sentiments of William Graham Sumner, America's foremost proponent of social Darwinism. In *What Social Classes Owe to Each Other* (1883), Sumner argued that the government owes the people a society in which the "best" men are allowed to realize their potential. Anything less is against the will of nature and an invitation to mediocrity.[21]

It is interesting to note that the civil service reformers did not advocate an elitist society. Many reform leaders respected the voting strength of the working classes. Edwin Godkin, a leading journalist and nineteenth-century reformer, argued against the creation of an officeholding aristocracy with the following:

In every country in the world the office-holder, like everybody else, bases his own opinion of himself and his office on the opinion of them entertained by the public. He thinks highly of them because his neighbors do. The Prussian or English civil or military officer bristles with the pride of station, largely because the public considers his station something to be proud of. So, also, in America, the office-holder does not bristle with pride of station because nobody thinks his station anything to be proud of. He is not kept humble by the insecurity of his tenure, but by the absence of popular reverence for his place. . . . One of the very odd things in the popular dread of an office holding aristocracy is that it arises out of the belief that an aristocracy can build itself up on self esteem simply.

But no aristocracy has ever been formed in any such way. It grows upon popular admission of its superiority, and not simply on its own estimates of itself. The attempts which have been occasionally made to create an aristocracy in new countries, or in countries in which the respect for station has died out, have always failed miserably for this reason.[22]

In this statement, Godkin is responding to and anticipating the critics of Tammany Hall and their immigrant supporters. The political reality of universal suffrage and the minority status of reform politicians forced the candidates to temper their enthusiasm for an exclusive form of government employment. The uneducated working-class voters were acutely aware of the inequities of their former government's civil service. They could not be expected to support the duplication of such a system.

By advocating a vertical recruitment system, the reformers reinforced and perpetuated the myth of upward social mobility. Downplaying the existence and importance of a social gentry or privileged class is one of the ironies of the reform movement in the nineteenth century. Most reformers, well educated and economically secure, neither needed nor wanted any position offered by the city. Thus they could afford to speak in abstract terms about jobs for which they were not potential applicants. In any case, the reformers had to continue the promotion of vertical recruitment if they were to sell their idea of merit.

In summary, the social Darwinist interpretation that the goal of the civil service, or merit system, to separate the best from the worst never attracted the public. The failures of the reelection bids of reform mayors suggest that the electorate had its doubts about the administration of the merit system and retained the notion that civil service choices were made on the basis of whom rather than on the basis of what one knows.

Another theme—the merit system as moral imperative—was also used to win converts to the movement. It was sometimes used simultaneously with the Darwinian concept, and at other times it was employed as a separate rallying cry.

MERIT AS A MORAL IMPERATIVE

The genteel reformers were the first to link the civil service reform movement to general ideas about natural rights (e.g., justice and freedom) and to the values of the Christian religion. Many who were attracted to the movement saw the merit system as a vehicle for purifying local government. Evangelizing for civil service reform became a labor of love for some of the city's leading citizens. Indeed, many prominent clergy-men in the nineteenth century supported the linkage of the merit system with religion. At a church congress in 1881, for example, the Reverend E. R. Atwell proclaimed:

We are here tonight to send a tributary into the great river, to manifest our opinion, to claim as part of that great American public that civil service shall be reformed. But someone will say, What has a Church Congress to do with such a question as this? Shall the Church, who has gloried in her ignoring of politics, descend from her high position? We reply: This is not a question of politics. It is a great moral question. It is a question which concerns the honor and honesty of the nation, a question intimately associated with the influences that form the character of a young man. It is a question which should interest every true patriot; and the more a man adds to patriotism of loyalty to God and the Church, the better qualified is he to advance the interests of reform.[23]

The enlistment of the clergy brought new life to a campaign that had many dull, moribund, and uninspiring adherents. The "new gospel" permeated the literature and speeches of the time, and politicians were compared to sinners, thieves, dupes, and other assorted misanthropes, a sort of description that continued until the turn of the century. The purpose of this campaign was (1) to legitimize the reform movement; (2) to identify the movement with leading citizens; and (3) to appeal to the working class's belief in religion. Henry Lambert, a leading member of the movement, observed that these objectives had been achieved. R. Fulton Cutting, a reformer, asserted that "the real crime committed against society by the spoils system is moral, not economic. It poisons our institutions at the fountainhead, corrupting the electorate and creating a political conscience antagonistic to morals."[24]

Lambert noted that of the 443 members of the New York Civil Service Association 55 were clergymen. Another dozen were professors or other notables; and the rest, businessmen. He argued that the working class should be represented because civil service reform had been intended to benefit them. In order to encourage working-class membership in the association, he wanted to reduce or eliminate membership fees. He also advocated the idea of an open competitive examination as a mechanism to create social mobility. In addition, he had a more practical plan:

Another way to influence the working classes is to issue brief broadsides, each bearing upon some one point, showing the values and importance of the movement to them. Tracts of even moderate length will find but few readers, while a brief page will receive attention. If by these brochures we can convince them that reform will be of some practical advantage to them, we shall have done much to secure their aid.[25]

The Lambert plan was never adopted, nor was it, it seems, ever a hot issue of debate within the movement. This is not surprising since few nineteenth-century social organizations were without class bias. Tammany's spokesmen criticized this, and rightly so, as evidence of an elitist posture on the part of the association leadership. The reformers were known to be altruistic but also to eschew contact with the working class. For many, the notion of an open society did not mean an end to class distinctions, but rather a better society for everyone.

The genteel reformers were not levelers—i.e., advocates of no social distinctions among men—but social humanitarians seeking to improve the lot of the less fortunate. On the surface this goal seems to be very enlightened, but the principle of equal opportunity alone does not guarantee everyone access to jobs and privileges. Recruiting a few working-class members for the association may have improved the Civil Service Reform Association's credibility with immigrant groups. The record shows, however, that the reformers were able to win the initial civil service victory without active participation by the working class.

Control of the municipal bureaucracy was a critical part of this campaign. The reformers wanted a system that would sort out the "best men" from the hordes of immigrants seeking public employment. Personnel choices based on talent alone would assure that the best-qualified applicants would get the job. Applicants would be hired on their own merits and would owe loyalty to no one. There would be no party bosses to pull strings in obtaining promotions or rescinding dismissals. Because the best men would prosper in such a setting, the result would yield a better administration.

This new brand of public employee would also serve as a moral example to the general public. In its supervisory role, the Civil Service Commission would ensure that the personnel arena would remain open and above partisanship. The commission would be the moral policeman for the government.

Reformers had other reasons, however, for wanting control of the municipal government. City Hall could be used as a forum for educating the immigrant voter. An editorial in the April 1883 edition of the *Civil Service Record*, entitled "Civil Reform in Municipal Government," is quite revealing:

The city of New York can roll up a majority which the rest of the state cannot overcome, and so may elect a president; but while its direct influence upon the nation is great, its indirect influence is far greater. If its government becomes corrupt the disease infects the whole body of politics. Tweed and Kelly have shown how easily a few unscrupulous men can dominate a million, and, one by one, all our great cities fall under the control of their worst classes.[26]

The position exemplified in the above excerpt identifies in part the dilemma of the reform movement. The reformers realized that the passage of a civil service law would not mean total success for their movement. Thus reformers' organizations had to become more politically involved to achieve this end. In so doing, they stood to lose their moral advantage over the political parties. In the same edition, the *Record* exhorts its readers to expose the corruption of the party leaders and to collect facts and make them public. The aim of this strategy was to show that the party leaders were enriching themselves at the expense of the public. The reformers, with the help of the press, accused party leaders of various criminal acts. They then promised the public a new civil service system, free from partisan politics and corruption.

The reformers proposed replacing the partisan personnel system with one based on merit principles. They believed that this would be in the public interest and would improve the quality of service. Such a system could even improve the quality of supervisors.

With better and abler men in subordinate places, mere politicians—mere strangers to its business, of any sort—would have a hard time indeed, when foisted over such subordinates to the head of a quiet office. They would be contemptible even in their own estimation. The bare fact that there were many able men in lower grades made it certain that the higher place would soon be filled with the lower.[27]

This quotation illustrates the visionary side of the reformers. They believed that a difficult examination would create a sense of accomplishment in the test takers. For this reason, the reformers stressed the use of questions that called for responses unrelated to work experience. In attempting to establish minimum literacy requirements, the objective was to make the selection process a quasi-intellectual trial. If an individual passed a civil service examination, it was supposedly an achievement in itself. In other words, examinations were designed to support and improve the image of public workers. The reformers did not attempt the creation of an administrative elite beyond any political manipulation, but rather aimed to create a group insulated from petty partisanship.

Later reformers attempted to impose a Max Weberian model (i.e., neutral competence) on city departments which would exclude the influence of political parties entirely. They believed that to select workers on the basis of merit would create a better environment and a more efficient government. Hiring would be based on intellectual potential rather than on work experience and technical qualifications. Although the reformers supported hierarchical organization, they considered the character of this bureaucratic leadership their highest priority. For them, remedies for the evils of the partisan or spoils bureaucracy were to be found in men, not structures. They wanted to recruit a whole class of public servants who owed their jobs to demonstrated intelligence. The performance of this new breed of workers would change the nature of municipal government. Vertical recruitment would be the key to good government.

In summary, the personnel system of the reformers was a social movement that captured the late nineteenth century liberal imagination. Reformers were convinced that the principle of incentive could motivate men in the business world. Applying these new notions of professionalism, the reformers wanted to introduce ethical standards into the thinking of public employees. Public employees would be offered life tenure for remaining apolitical. Finally, the advocates of the partisan personnel system proved to be competent adversaries for the reformers. Tammany candidates succeeded in preventing reform mayors from winning second terms. Once the members of the partisan bureaucracy returned to power, they totally ignored the rules established by the reformers.

MERIT: The Opposite of Patronage

The civil service reform movement started as a struggle against the spoils system, party patronage, or what Professor Lucius Wilmerding has called "eleemosynary appointments."[28] These charitable appointments were not free of obligation. Indeed workers who received jobs were expected to pay a fee for the privilege of working. The fees went into the party coffers and helped finance both electoral as well as social work activities.

Party patronage in nineteenth-century New York was a complex of reciprocal relationships. Many of these relationships could not be duplicated today, but some continue as part of the incentive system of political parties. For this reason Professor James Q. Wilson's definition of patronage is appropriate to our discussion:

All forms of material benefits which a politician may distribute to party workers and supporters. . . . Patronage jobs are all those posts, distributed at the discretion of political leaders, the pay for which is greater, than the value of the public services performed.[29]

The reform literature of the nineteenth century defines patronage as the practice of awarding public employment to supporters of political parties without regard to qualification. Under such a system, party loyalty is rewarded at the expense of intellectual achievement or job performance. Public employees can be dismissed arbitrarily and their wages assessed for partisan purposes. For reformers, patronage always led to corruption, inefficiency, and bossism. The reformers promised to eliminate patronage entirely. Once in office, many reformers found that patronage was a necessary incentive to induce individuals to continue to participate in reform parties. The reformers then began to advocate regulating rather than eliminating patronage. A *Civil Service Record* editorial asserts:

With our city patronage once regulated, and the selection of all employees and laborers taken out of politics, we shall begin a new era in municipal government; and that will effect more permanent good results than many citizen's meetings, citizen tickets, and new charter, and the whole series of past discouraging efforts for reform of city politics. Not that it will do away with all the need of effort on the part of our *best* citizens, but it will give us a better hope of good results, and will remove the great weight of patronage which we push and work against and sometimes see rolled into place, but only to have it rolled back again on us for the moment.[30]

Appointing reformers to high office was regarded as somehow different from patronage. Tammany's patronage was that well-known practice of selling jobs, giving bribes, and committing other kinds of petty crimes. Reformers portrayed the Tweed gang, which employed systematic patronage, as the acme of corruption. The investigation and criminal conviction of the Tweed gang and its later progeny, the Fassett (1890), Lexow (1894), Mazet (1899), and Seabury (1931) corruption committee investigations, were used by the reformers as evidence of the abuses of patronage that the merit system would prevent. It was claimed that the patronage system encouraged the recruitment of incompetent and dishonest public servants. Under this system, the argument ran, city workers bought their jobs and paid a fee to keep them. The political party retained the power to hire and fire employees at its whim. Aside from the political assessments and party prestidigitation within city government, Tammany was accused of committing crimes with impunity. The reformers claimed that reform was only possible with the elimination of such partisan patronage. Note the following:

The practical method of preventing favoritism, a method which has been aptly justified by experience, is the selection of non-political employees of government by a wise system of competition and probation. This method would not only secure the most intelligent public agents and those best fitted for the special duty required, but it would at once deprive leading politicians, of high and low degree, of the means of their ignoble traffic. It would prevent arbitrary removals, because the object of such removals, which is to substitute one particular person for another, would disappear. It would stop political assessments by leaving employees equal liberty with all other citizens to give or withhold, a liberty which is both illogical and impossible under the spoils system. It would tend to correct the sycophancy, terror, suffering, and demoralization within the service, and the public extravagance, corruption and danger bred by the present system, by striking at its source.[31]

This notion of an antipatronage model is very similar to the moral basis of merit, which maintains that the merit system will somehow deliver public employees from evil. It is interesting that the reformers retained the same visionary posture when they entered the real world of partisan politics, the state legislature, in search of a municipal civil service law.

The reformers defined partisan patronage as an evil political tool used by ineffective and unqualified politicians to retain power and obtain reelection. When they discussed patronage, they referred to entry-level managerial positions, unskilled labor, and clerical, public-safety, and custodial jobs. The filling of these jobs may be described as petty patronage; that is, they are jobs for which the upwardly mobile working and middle classes are not applicants.

These jobs are distinct from those that require little manual skill, such as those of high-level administrators, teachers, social workers, engineers. The latter require training and are generally self-selective. They are considered middle-class jobs, and are among the most sought-after in municipal government. As the middle class began to control such positions, they developed a new system of patronage. If the old patronage system operated by Tammany Hall is considered petty patronage, then the new system may be termed grand patronage.

Grand patronage includes those positions above the middle-management level. The upwardly mobile working and middle classes seek these jobs as a source of income and status. The following positions may be conceived as belonging to this category: commissionerships, deputy commissionerships, memberships on advisory and governing boards, judgeships, and staff positions in central offices. Chart 2.1 shows how the two types of patronage differ.

Chart 2.1 suggests a critical difference between the old and new forms of patronage. The new spoilsmen can select from a relatively limited pool of candidates and be assured that the minimum job qualifications will be met. The chart also suggests that qualifications, although necessary, are not the only requirements for a new patronage job. Merit then, in this sense, emerges not just as an alternative to the patronage system, but

CHART 2.1

Petty Patronage	Grand Patronage
Loyalty to party	Loyalty to interest group or professional associations
Appointment by party official	Appointment by elected official commission or search committee
Low credential requirements	High credential requirements
Standard and continuous political assessment	Only preappointment assessment required
Prefer temporary appointment	Prefer life or term tenure
Prefer ethnic distribution	Eschew ethnic distribution
Prefer long ballot	Prefer short ballot
Prefer performance test	Prefer written test
Informal working agreements	Formal contracts
Eschew organizational conflict	Accept conflict as normal
Allocate jobs through party organization	Allocate jobs through social network

as a means of restricting applicants. Professors William E. Mosher and J. Donald Kingley recognized this possibility when they noted the dual function of a Civil Service Commission. According to them, it may "keep the rascal out or may guard in such a way that only those with the requisite amount of political merit may enter."[32] The new job requirements may also improve, as history has shown, the quality of the applicant pool. Job seekers may acquire more education in order to improve eventually their position chances.

Three main themes have emerged from this discussion of the merit system. First, it is impossible to separate the objective aspects of the system from its function within a given context. Second, the use of the merit system as a political tool is designed to protect the interest of the dominant social class. Third, the invocation of the word "merit" in a political discussion aims to convince an audience of the soundness of the speaker's or writer's argument. It serves as a perfect mask for political motives. The history of the New York City civil service movement suggests that its advocates were successful in using the phrase to promote their own interests.

The reformers were not, however, entirely successful in keeping charges of partisan influence out of their handling of city politics. They had to endure reproachments from the regular political parties as well as from organized interest groups, which challenged the reformers on questions of grand patronage and forced concessions concerning the representation of all members of society in the allocation of these new spoils.

The writer Harry Kranz's commentary on the merit principle is an appropriate summary for this section of this chapter:

Throughout American history, the concept of "merit" in public employment has had a rubbery texture, stretching or contracting to cover the prevailing ethos, but at no time either before or after adoption of the civil service reforms of the 1880's has actual merit (defined as the ability to perform specific jobs) prevailed as the predominant or exclusive method of selecting the American bureaucracy.[33]

If the merit system is to remain a tool of ascending groups, it must retain its elastic quality. Otherwise, it will lose its persuasive powers in the personnel community.

REFORM POLITICS AND THE PASSAGE OF THE CIVIL SERVICE ACT

The political momentum generated by the passage in Congress of the Pendleton Act of 1883, which established a national civil service system, spilled over into state politics. Dorman Eaton, a prominent New York City lawyer, was the architect of this ground-breaking legislation. A few years prior to its enactment, in May 1877, the National Civil Service Reform League had been founded in New York, and New Yorkers like Everett Wheeler, George William Curtis, Edwin Godkin, Dorman Eaton, John Jay, and Silas Burt had already established national reputations as civil service reformers.[34] Still, the city that produced these famous reformers also provided, as discussed above, the political environment for the development of the nation's best-known political machine—Tammany Hall. As one writer has observed, New York was "home alike of the active innovators and of the most odious bosses."[35]

Once the reformers had won the national struggle for a federal civil service, they turned their sights on the states and municipalities. Hoogenboom's study suggests, however, that the movement began to disintegrate after the initial victory.[36] His analysis is correct for the national picture, but on the municipal level, men who had played minor or secondary roles in the national arena threw themselves into local politics. The job of reforming the state and municipal employee systems had little glamour attached to it, and a high probability of failure. The giants of the reform movement, such as George William Curtis and Carl Schurz, left the local job to people like Everett Wheeler, Edward Shepard, and Edwin Godkin.[37] The New York reformers knew that the "state house gangs" had control of the state legislature and would resist any form of civil service however mild or benign.

The *Civil Service Record,* the official newspaper of the National Civil Service League, under the heading "Civil Service in State and City" editorially exhorted its readers to launch a battle on the local level similar to the national one. The paper suggested that state civil service was not so large but just as critical an arena, and therefore as genuine a target for reform, as the federal government. The article asked:

Would not neglecting to reform the state civil service, because its evils are not on so great a scale as the evils in the national civil service, which we have just begun to reform, be very like refusing to stop a leak in the boat in which we are rowing, because a bigger hole in some big ship sailing within sight of us has been nearly closed? Let "thorough" be our motto.[38]

Because most New York reformers were independent Republicans, they expected more legislative assistance from fellow Republicans, but a weak local party organization constrained their efforts. In order to get a state civil service law passed, they had to hold the upstate Republican machine and the liberal Republicans together and win the independent Democrats to their side. The city's Democratic machine—Tammany—should have been able to find an ally or at least a sympathizer in the upstate Republican political machine, but patronage rivalry between the two organizations prevented any cooperation and aided the legislative success of the reformers.

New York City was not only a symbol of a recalcitrant and corrupt political machine but also a test case for the reformers who aspired to root out evil from every American city. In their appeal for the new civil service, the genteel reformers emphasized a benign, nonpartisan change that would improve public service without taking away political control of cities from the local parties. Among the political conditions in 1883 that facilitated the strategy of the civil service reformers were (1) the uncertainty created by the defeat of the Democratic party in 1883; (2) the election of an ambitious and anti-Tammany Democrat—Grover Cleveland—as governor of the state of New York; (3) the relative strength of the reform Republican leadership in the state legislature; e.g., Theodore Roosevelt; (4) the election of Mayor Franklin Edson, a candidate of both the reform-oriented County Democrats and the regular Tammany Democrats; and (5) the uncertain leadership of "Honest" John Kelly.

The Tammany Democrats, its candidate having lost the mayoralty race in 1878, the governorship in 1879, and the presidential race in 1880, had to reestablish its reputation as a winner or see its influence wane in city politics. Kelly needed a victory, and his first move after the 1883 gubernatorial election was to coax a patronage commitment from Governor Cleveland.

Patronage, the lifeblood of any political machine, was needed as an incentive for party recruitment, participation, and support. Historians Alfred Connable and Edward Silberfarb have observed that "the key to Tammany's effectiveness under Boss Kelly was, of course, the ability to win elections by dispensing personal favors to the voters and party workers, thereby controlling more public offices to dispense more favors. This system of self-perpetuation was a smaller and more intimate precursor of the New Deal."[39]

Kelly was unable to get Cleveland's commitment on patronage, nor could he resist the movement toward a Pendleton-type civil service act for the state, although he was briefly successful in slowing the bill's progress by making an appearance in Albany. He attempted to outmaneuver a coalition made up of reformers and independent Democrats, but the legislature finally passed the bill jointly sponsored by the Civil Service Association and the independent Democrats, initially introduced by Jacob Miller of New York.

The Adoption of the Civil Service System. Following the injustices and deficiencies of patronage and the undermining of partisan control of the New York City bureaucracy in 1883, the introduction of the merit system was more than a victory over Tammany Hall; it was a triumph for vertical recruitment. The institutionalization of this form of employment insured a pliant civil service, and at the same time, the promotion of middle-class values.

The impetus for nineteenth-century civil service reform emanated from what has been characterized as the rampant corruption of municipal government under the control of Tammany Hall. After the Civil War, industrialists assumed a more active role in public affairs. The involvement of businessmen in politics began with the mercantile capitalists, who maintained a working relationship with local politicians but who never endorsed the tactics of Tammany. The rise of industrial capitalists, along with the conviction of Boss Tweed in 1873, signaled the end of partisan control of the city administration. The new capitalists abrogated their alliance with the political machine, and sought respectability by aligning themselves with the forces of reform. The reformers promised a moral revival through good management and nonpartisan government. Ten years after Boss Tweed's conviction, New York became the first state in the Union to enact a civil service law. The loose brand of Jacksonian democracy, with its emphasis on patronage jobs for political supporters, was replaced by a new politics based on nonpartisan moralism.

THE TRIUMPH OF GENTEEL REFORM

On April 8, 1883, when the New York State Legislature passed the first statewide civil service law, Section 8 of Chapter 314 provided for the establishment of a municipal Civil Service Commission for cities with a population of more than 50,000. Mayor Franklin Edson accordingly met in September of that year with the newly established state Civil Service Commission and agreed to promulgate the first municipal rules and regulations for a New York City civil service. Shortly afterward, he asked Everett Wheeler to write the city's first civil service rules and regulations. Although these rules were simple compared to today's standards, they became the guidelines for a new system of recruiting public employees. Wheeler and Edwin Godkin, the publisher of the *Nation,* served as civil service commissioners in the administrations of Mayors Edson, Abram Hewitt, and William Grace. They wrote and rewrote the requirements for new employees, but were not entirely successful in weeding out the partisan practices of Tammany Hall.

In the mayoralty race of 1894, the reformers and many Republicans supported the candidacy of William Strong, who tried to extend the ideas of reform to all the city's agencies. Strong also made the Civil Service Commission a coequal agency in his informal cabinet system of government. With the help of Everett Wheeler, Strong's administration gained a national reputation as a showcase for reform government. One of his cabinet luminaries was the flamboyant General George Waring, the street commissioner. Waring dressed his workers in white uniforms, and they became known as "Waring's White Wings." He considered that his men in their white uniforms exemplified the reform model of the new municipal employee. About them he said:

What has really been done has been to put a man instead of a voter at the end of the broom-handle. The "White Wings" are by no means white angels, but they are a splendid body of men, a body on which the people of New York can depend for any needed service, without regard to hours or personal comfort. A trusted sweeper, for example, will stand on a windy dock-log all night long, and night after night, protecting the city against the wiles and tricks of the snow-carters. He gets no extra pay for this, but his extra service and his hardship are compensated by the consciousness that he is doing good work, that his good work is appreciated by his officers, and that the force to which he belongs is winning public favor partly because of what he himself is doing. In other words, the whole department is activated by a real *esprit de corps,* without which no organization of men can do its best, either in war or in peace.[40]

The foregoing illustrates the philosophy of the genteel reformers. They envisioned a new type of public employee who would be efficient, hardworking, incorruptible, and responsive to good leadership. By eliminating political assessments and arbitrary dismissals, the reformers sought to build loyalty by moral example. A "good" man could enter the civil service and rise as far as his energy and intelligence would take him. Vertical recruitment was not just a concept, but a crusade to demonstrate the superiority of moral government.

With the defeat of William Strong in 1897, the genteel reformers lost direct control of the development of the city personnel system. They managed, however, to retain indirect control through the governor's office, the state legislature, and the courts. Although the reformers thus continued to win the overall war with Tammany Hall, they soon lost the local battle for the electorate. Tammany Hall did not hesitate to use its elaborate social and political networks against the reformers. To counterbalance this strategy, reformers relied on the personality and rhetoric of their candidates.

The defeat of Strong came at a critical time for the nation as well as the city. In Henry Steele Commager's words, the decade of the 1890s was a "watershed of American history."[41] The United States was in a period of ideological restlessness and industrial development. With this political and economic metamorphosis came a new class of workers who by their sheer numbers posed a problem for the new economic elite. Winning the allegiance of this new group of workers was critical to the reform movement's moral crusade and the new industrialist's attempt to legitimize economic change.

In order to achieve and institutionalize their values, the reformers had to control the office of the mayor. For this purpose, they created a municipal-reform association, Citizens Union, and began to compete in local elections with the two major parties. Their initial support was given to Seth Low, the former mayor of Brooklyn who was then president of Columbia University, in his bid to be the city's mayor. Low lost the race, and Robert Van Wyck, with the strong backing of Tammany Hall, became the first mayor of Greater New York City, which then included the five present boroughs with a population of 3,393,252.[42]

The reformers had lost control of City Hall at a moment when the powers of the mayor had been greatly increased by the new consolidated charter. Under this charter, the city no longer needed state approval to promulgate new civil service regulations. In 1898, the Van Wyck administration appointed commissioners who rewrote the entire set of civil service guidelines in order to render them more acceptable to the needs of Tammany Hall. They replaced the eligibility list with a position list, which meant that temporary appointments could be made in every department. The departments were now as regressive as they had been before the enactment of the consolidation charter, meaning that it was again possible to hire individuals regardless of their place on a waiting list. The Van Wyck changes, although modified somewhat at the insistence of the state Civil Service Commission, undid most of the work of the genteel reformers and again made partisan politics the basis for recruitment.

The reformers had lost another battle but once more not the war, for they began to attack the Van Wyck administration in the state courts. In 1899 they were successful in getting the state legislature to establish the Mazet committee, which found widespread criminal activities in many city departments. These disclosures and the resulting scandal provided the impetus for a new city charter, which set the stage again for the return of reformers to City Hall. In his second attempt at the mayoralty, Seth Low was elected, and he and his fellow reformers tried to reverse the damage inflicted upon the civil service by the Tammany-inspired Van Wyck administration. This proved to be an impossible task as the new charter had reduced the administrative power of the mayor.

Under the charter revision of 1901, the borough presidents were given control over the administration of their boroughs, while the Board of Estimate and Apportionments was given independent status as a second branch of the city legislature. Nevertheless, the mayor still controlled the municipal Civil Service Commission, and that body set forth new rules which on December 4, 1903, reinstituted the vertical system of recruitment. George Elcaness, in his history of the city Civil Service Commission, has commented that

the Low Commission had much to do, following as it did, upon the heels of a commission which would rather have seen the merit system destroyed. In the years the Low Civil Service Commission functioned, it accomplished much of value. It instituted a regrading and reclassification system which, while not as thorough as could be desired, nevertheless was needed. The staff of the full-time examiners was also increased in an effort to speed up the work of conducting the numerous examinations which were held.[43]

Although the Low commission worked hard, it lacked the creative leadership of Everett Wheeler, who had become ill during Low's term in office. The courts also hurt the Low administration's attempts at reform by granting civil service exemptions to the offices of registrar, sheriff, and county clerk. The momentum brought about by the Mazet investigation into corrupt department practices failed to affect the outcome of the 1903 election, and the reformers once again lost to Tammany. Lincoln Steffens, the muckraker, and the reformers, believed that Low's cold and impersonal manner failed to win him the public support that he needed for reelection. In this respect, Steffens called Mayor Low a "bourgeois, reformer type."[44]

SUMMARY

The epoch of the Low administration was critical in the city's civil service history, for it marked the end of "aristocratic" intervention into the workings of the municipal Civil Service Commission. Low's administration was the "last hurrah" for the genteel reformers. It also saw the exit of Everett Wheeler, the father of the city's first civil service system. Wheeler and his colleagues had been a major influence in New York politics from 1883 to 1902. They had attempted, although unsuccessfully, to achieve the goal of building a nonpartisan civil service based on merit principles. It was a vision of a meritocracy free of immorality and criminality.

3

ACADEMIC REFORMERS
AND THE POLITICS
OF MAYORALTY CONTROL

The failures of the Low administration may have caused many genteel reformers to lose faith in the powers of elected mayors. The mayor seemed to have too many rivals for power and too few opportunities to assert the mission of his administration. Thus the solution to weak mayorality government was to eliminate all elected officials except the mayor (i.e., the short ballot movement) and restrict mayoral action in the day-to-day activities of government (i.e., the city-manager concept).

The Low administration had proved that personality and conviction were insufficient deterrents to inefficient government. A weak mayor, regardless of his convictions, was at the mercy of an entrenched bureaucracy. The alternative to a weak mayor was a mayor with absolute power over city affairs. For these reformers absolute power brought with it the propensity to abuse it. The failure of the Low administration therefore placed the genteel reformers on the horns of a dilemma. If they continued to support a weak mayorality form of government, they ran the risk of losing control of administration and would further damage their candidates' chances of getting reelected. If they supported a strong mayorality form of government, they ran the risk of a patronage stampede. Such a policy might insure reelection but would compromise their moral posture and expose them to the petty politics of municipal administration.

Volunteering to steer through the horns of the dilemma came a new group of reformers. This group was composed of Progressives, university professors, government researchers, consultants, and social workers. They proposed that the reform movement cease its emphasis on morality and concentrate on the empowerment of the chief executive. The patronage stampede could be avoided by relegating petty patronage to the classified civil service. The elected mayor would not hold any sway over petty patronage. The exempt positions would be reserved for grand patronage. This paronage could be controlled by restricting vertical recruitment and increasing the education requirements for top municipal jobs.

The genteel reformers were prepared to give the new reformers an opportunity to test their ideas. They created the Bureau of Municipal Research—now the Institute of Public Administration—to conduct studies of city departments. They continued to support the bureau financially and encouraged the recruitment of university-trained researchers. The new reformers in turn assumed the leadership of the movement. The new crusaders had three objectives: (1) to separate politics from local government administration; (2) to create an autonomous managerial class of professionals; and (3) to introduce new managerial techniques into the bureaucracy.

For these reformers efficient government could be achieved by removing the organizational slack caused by partisan politics and fragmentation of administrative authority. In order to assume managerial control, power, authority, and responsibility had to be consolidated in the mayor's office. Managing the government from City Hall required more political leverage over departments. The new reformers became advocates of executive-centered government and the application of scientific management.

Unlike their wealthy predecessors—the genteel reformers—the new group saw government as a potential source of employment. The genteel reformers were never interested in jobs below a city commissionership or a seat on the Civil Service Commission. They served in government only out of a sense of duty. For this reason Mayor Strong had difficulty recruiting individuals for the city's top positions. The academic reformers, on the other hand, were interested in commissionships, but they also wanted jobs deep in the deputy-commissioner and middle-management ranks. In order to secure those jobs for professionally trained persons, the academic reformers sought to expand grand patronage and insulate it from the election process.

Academic reformers, like their predecessors, knew the importance of gaining the mayoralty. Winning elections was difficult because Tammany Hall was able to recruit more attractive candidates. Charles F. Murphy, the new leader of Tammany, persuaded George B. McClellan, son of the famous Civil War general, to run against Mayor Low. McClellan was elected and inaugurated a new era of moderation toward civil service reform. He began by acting like a reform mayor. For example, he dismissed the entire Civil Service Commission for violating civil service law. No reform administration could boast of such a coup.

McClellan was able to reduce the number of exempt positions without alienating Tammany Hall. They supported his reelection in 1905 and 1907. In 1909 McClellan attempted the ultimate coup: the removal of Tammany Hall's influence in municipal politics. Murphy was able to resist this move and replaced McClellan with William Gaynor.

Mayor Gaynor, elected in 1909, immediately proceeded to knock four hundred Tammany politicians off the city payroll. What is more, he pledged himself to reinstitute vertical recruitment and nonpartisan government, and even tried to establish a residency law for civil servants. These efforts failed, but historians credit Gaynor as a catalyst for change by citing, among other things, his having revived the monthly cabinet meetings, begun during the administration of William L. Strong, which attempted to support the autonomy of department heads by promoting interdepartmental relations and downgrading party influence.

Gaynor supported the Civil Service Commission, ruling that all appointments and promotions should be made in numerical order from a competitive list. He forbade civil servants to join political clubs. The new mayor, in effect, double-crossed Tammany and gained a reputation as an enemy of partisan politics. For these anti-Tammany tactics, he was dubbed "the Tammany Mayor who swallowed the Tiger."

Louis H. Pink, the mayor's biographer, saw the first few months of the Gaynor administration as revolutionizing municipal government.[1] New York could remain the center of municipal reform even with a Tammany-backed Mayor. All this changed when scandal and an attempt on Gaynor's life blunted the force of the mayor's reforms. Following the assassination attempt, Gaynor's lack of interest in government reform was not surprising, for he had weakened the Tammany patronage system and had given his adopted reformers a theme for the next election.

The McClellen and Gaynor administrations proved that a mayor could defy the party and impose administrative reforms from City Hall. The reforms were implemented without abuses of petty patronage. Nevertheless the academic reformers were interested in more than launching anti-Tammany campaigns. They wanted to change the nature of the civil service and introduce the concept of scientific management.

THE TRIUMPH OF MIDDLE-CLASS REFORM

The opportunity to put into practice the academic reformers' ideas came with the election of John Purroy Mitchel in 1914. At the age of thirty-four, Mitchel combined the forces of the independent Democrats and the Republicans in order to gain election as the second fusion mayor in New York City history. Mitchel had been associated with the reform movement and was a convert to the efficient-government movement.

Mitchel's administration represents a significant epoch in city history because his staff repudiated vertical recruitment and examination procedures in civil service. Robert Moses, a young staff member at the Bureau of Municipal Research, became one of the leading advocates for a change in the system.

In his 1914 Ph.D. dissertation Moses attacked Dorman Eaton's notion of an open and vertical recruitment system. He did not believe that competitive examinations could produce a body of high-caliber managers. Moses felt that examinations made only simple "mathematical and palpable"[2] distinctions between men, and that such a random-selection process was too unreliable for the management needs of modern society. He stated:

As a civil service reformer Mr. Eaton's work deserves the highest praise. It is something to have set up an honest, competitive civil service, though its standard be the truly democratic one of uniform mediocrity; but such democracy is false democracy, and until we have a service which attracts the elite of our young men, trained for intellectual work and on a higher level than mechanical clerks, we shall have no civil service worthy of the name.[3]

This attack on vertical recruitment reflects Moses' preference for the British method of selecting an administrative class as well as his rather deep conviction that the American system of recruitment had outgrown its usefulness. He felt that the demands of a growing city required a professional corps of highly trained managers to provide the efficient administration needed by the city. Hiring from within the city departments would not insure competent applicants. Why take a chance on hiring good candidates when one could easily organize a system that would recruit managers based on talent? The lateral entrance of individual recruits at all levels of government would lead to hiring the best people. Those who entered the organization fresh from the outside would possess fewer political ties and be better equipped to make changes in the agencies. Moses advocated a new horizontal recruitment system that would provide a vehicle for later entrance of outsiders and open the managerial stratum to change.

This new horizontal system would assure that the "best" people were no longer wasting their time coming up through the ranks. The recruits would immediately assume the roles for which they were qualified. For instance, a man out of college with an interest in and qualifications for a management job would start as a junior manager rather than as an administrative clerk.

The proponents of horizontal recruitment also advocated a tracking system that would put a ceiling on the career mobility of lower-ranking civil service employees, so that they would never be promoted beyond a certain point. The high-level administrators would be recruited from the outside. In other words, the competition for certain jobs would be restricted to men within the same talent brackets. A candidate would compete only with others possessing the same educational and technical qualifications.

The genteel reformers must be defined in light of the previous discussion. The elitist theme that the genteel reformers sought to avoid reappeared with the academic reformers who then sought city jobs. The reemergence of this theme in the writing of these new reformers signaled the end of the myth that there are good people in city government who simply need to be freed of their political affiliations. The proponents of horizontal recruitment argued that only personnel recruited from the outside could save the bureaucracy from its inefficient ways.

The idea of a well-trained administrative class was not new, for in 1887 Woodrow Wilson, then a young instructor in history at Bryn Mawr College, had pointed out that "administrative questions are not political questions."[4] Wilson's thinking underscored that of the academic reformers, namely that politicians should not manipulate or dictate to administrators. Thirteen years later, in *Politics and Administration,* Professor Frank Goodnow supported the separation of administration and politics as follows:

There is a large part of administration which is unconnected with politics, which should therefore be relieved very largely, if not altogether, from the control of political bodies. It is unconnected with politics because it embraces fields of semi-scientific, *quasi*-judicial and *quasi*-business or commercial activities—work which has little if any influence on the expression of the true state will.[5]

It was actually Frederick W. Taylor—an industrial engineer—and the "Taylorites" who had a major influence on Mitchel and his academic reformers. Taylor in a paper entitled "A Piece-Rate System, Being a Step Toward a Partial Solution of the Labor Problem" outlined the belief that work could be organized scientifically. The paper was presented before the American Society of Mechanical Engineers in 1895.[6] Taylor's later works, including the famous *Principles of Scientific Management*, can be read as an attempt to replace the wage system with a differentiated and individualized incentive system.[7] His treatise was a twofold response to the increasing labor costs of industrial workers and to the threat of labor unions.

Taylorism was an attempt to apply the scientific methods and tools of engineering to work habits, and the movement's advocates were appropriately dubbed Taylorites. Taylor believed that every job could be performed in a certain period of time and reorganized to save man-hour costs and resources. He thought that workers, released from the pressure of a foreman presiding over them, would produce to their fullest capacity. Efficiency could be introduced into any operation by systematizing the work. By breaking down each job into its basic functions, he thought, ways could be found to increase worker output.

But Taylorism went further than advocating the restriction of foremen and supervisors. According to Taylor, workers should be treated as individuals, and rewarded or punished accordingly. Taylor and his disciples believed in the standardization of parts and the development of a strong department of planning. They also thought that the work area should be a moral gymnasium celebrating the middle-class notion of individual achievement. Taylorites organized themselves into "the Efficiency Society" and published *Efficiency Magazine*. In an article for this publication, Mayor Mitchel asserted:

Once the city government begins to feel the exhilaration of accomplishment, it is not difficult to increase the effectiveness of work and the enthusiasm of employees or to substitute economy for slovenly expenditures, but it is a bigger problem to find out how to redefine and redirect the work of health, police, corrections, charities, and school departments so that we can pave the way for a better city life, as well as deal with day-to-day necessities. This is what we are trying to do in New York under the present administration—not only working out the "how" of city government, but the "what" of city government activities as well. This is the big problem of efficiency.[8]

The academic elite showered the Mitchel administration with praise. Charles Beard, then a Columbia University historian who later became director of the Bureau of Municipal Research, thought that Mitchel was the ideal politician because he had the courage to introduce changes in administration without fear for his political career. Beard, who was also impressed with the attention Mitchel gave to problems, has written:

Perhaps the most significant feature of Mr. Mitchel's administration was the businesslike management of the millions of details involving the funds, property, and employees of the city—the elimination of petty wastes at a thousand point, the selection of able people to discharge even the smallest duties, the persistent watchfulness at points far and wide, like the watchfulness of privates in a great army, each of whom feels his sense of personal responsibility and has confidence in the high command.[9]

The Taylorites were divided into two basic groups. The systematizers—accountants, engineers, and managers—drew their analogy for work reorganization from machines and the military. Following the credo of the Protestant work ethic, they believed that hard work yielded morality. The industrial betterment proponents—the second Taylorite group—drew most of their inspiration from social-betterment work. They fought for humane working conditions. John H. Patterson, of the National Cash Register Company and the dominant figure in this movement, believed that employees who had such things as lunchrooms, clinics, and safety-training programs would be more productive. According to this view, a happy laborer would produce more goods and would eschew unions. In other words, it was thought that morality and provision for the worker's well-being would produce hard work and higher levels of production.[10]

Mitchel was influenced by advocates of the systematizer and social-betterment groups. Henry Bruère, Mitchel's top assistant and a systematizer, William H. Allen, and Frederick Cleveland established the first management-consultant and research organization, later known as the Bureau of Municipal Research. This organization grew out of the Citizens Union-sponsored study of bureau administration in Manhattan. This municipal study group, then called the Bureau of City Betterment, published a tract—*How Manhattan is Governed: Illustrated with 58 Photographs and Drawings;* documenting the mismanagement of street and sewer repairs, it made the bureau famous.

John A. Kingbury, Henry Moskowitz, and Katherine B. Davis, leading social workers under Mitchel, had been on the staff of the Association for Improving the Condition of the Poor. They felt that an efficient city would result in efficient citizens, and that improved social services and public amenities would create the environment for citizen development. But their work was overshadowed by that of Frederick Cleveland and Robert Moses. Cleveland promoted the idea of budgetary reform, while Moses conducted the first comprehensive study of the city bureaucracy. Their work laid the foundation for the Mitchel administration's experiment in city government.

Moses and a small staff undertook a "scientific-management" analysis of the city's departments. After the study, Moses proposed a system that synthesized his elitist notions of managerial talents and Taylorism. Like most scientific-management prescriptions, the plan advocated a complete overhaul of procedures, performance evaluations, and administrative structure. It focused on work methods and ways to increase the efficiency of employees. But after reading Moses' analysis, Robert Caro, his biographer, thought that it was Calvinistic and represented "the proposals of a fanatic."[11]

Actually the Moses tract was a masterpiece of scientific management. If his proposals had been enacted, Moses might have accomplished in the public sector what Frederick Taylor claimed to have done in the private one. Developing a model for greater productivity within city departments would have involved reorganizing, redesigning, and re-thinking the entire work ethos among city employees. Moses proposed a flat rate for all clerical workers. They would be able to increase their pay by demonstrating their skill and productivity. The Moses proposal would end fixed salaries and automatic increments based on seniority. Not surprisingly, Moses' ideas were not received with enthusiasm by the city's civil servants. This may have been one of the reasons why Mayor Mitchel decided not to institute the Moses' plan for reorganization.

In 1915, the New York State Civil Service Commission accused Mitchel's commissioners of appointing friends to jobs in violation of civil service rules. The commission documented a series of such violations, one of which involved Teachers College professor E. L. Thorndike, who had been asked by the Civil Service Commission to recommend applicants for a position in the Department of Education.

Burdette R. Buckingham, one of the applicants, was a former student of Thorndike's. Aware that Buckingham had taken the examination, Thorndike recognized the handwriting, but he did not disqualify himself and recommended his former student for the job. The state commissioners believed that this was against civil service regulations; they claimed that the violation was the result of the Mitchel administration's "mania for efficiency"; i.e., demanding efficiency at the expense of civil service rules.

In another widely reported case, an "efficiency engineer" was hired without an examination and was allowed to work beyond the time limits set for temporary personnel. After questioning the engineer, John Mann, the commission concluded that "the witness is employed as an 'expert' on work which is *new* to him and of which he *had no knowledge whatever prior to his service to the city,* and civil service rules *were violated,* in two particulars by the municipal commission, to continue his employment."[12]

In 1916 the Bureau of Municipal Research produced a report critical of the Mitchel administration's progress in reforming the civil service. The report described the municipal civil service as chaotic, and stated that the entire classification, examination, and compensation systems were in need of revision. Record keeping was poor and lacked statistical data and appropriate filing procedures. The Mitchel administration was able to correct this and made some meaningful changes in the system. It hired outside examiners to conduct tests for senior-grade positions and advertising experts that would improve the recruitment process. This was the first time that paid experts from the private sector had been brought into the recruitment process. It was the dawn of the age of the itinerant urban specialist.

The Mitchel administration had started off with great hopes for reform, but it failed to win the support of the civil servants, and Mitchel's political fate was similar to that of reform mayors Strong and Low. Neither could they institutionalize their reforms nor could they generate any public support for their changes in civil service policy. The Moses plan was a good example of misreading the interests and attitudes of public employees. Civil servants resisted Taylorism for the same reasons that factory workers did. Taylorism would, in short, change the way they worked. More important, it preached a kind of leveling philosophy that undermined seniority, foreman-supervisor prerogatives, and fixed-pay scales. Robert Moses helped to politicize civil servants by attempting to sell the plan at public meetings. His failure, once again, created a temporary coalition of Tammany Hall and the civil servants.

Mitchel was not reelected. The next twenty years saw Tammany trying to capitalize on the demise of the academic reformers, only to misread the changing political situation.

MAYORAL EMPOWERMENT THROUGH ENTREPRENEURSHIP

After a succession of Tammany-backed mayors who did little to strengthen the office's managerial capacity, the city was ready for a dynamic leader. Fiorello H. LaGuardia, popularly known as "the Little Flower," became the fourth reform and fusion mayor since the passage of the New York State Civil Service Law in 1883. The combined factors of the Seabury investigation, of the Great Depression, and of LaGuardia himself made possible the fusion victory of 1933.[13]

Mayor LaGuardia met the challenge of a fragmented and economically depressed city government with a flamboyant personal style of administrative leadership. Unlike the three fusion mayors who preceded him, LaGuardia personally intervened in the affairs of the Civil Service Commission. He established a new classification system in 1934 and reorganized the commission. He reduced the number of exemptions and noncompetitive positions. William P. Brown, a New York University political scientist, cites an increase of from 54.5 to 75.25 percent in civil-service employees in competitive positions under LaGuardia.[14] The mayor was as aggressive in the field of civil service as he was in other areas of politics.

Charles Belous, a journalist, believes that LaGuardia brought a new "esprit de corps" to municipal government.[15] The mayor attempted to get the Civil Service Commission to develop examinations for all occupational titles. LaGuardia was the first mayor to advocate public service as a career for college graduates. For his campaign he drew upon the services of academic reformers. Professors Norman Powell and Wallace Sayre served as civil service commissioners in the LaGuardia administration. Many academic-reform ideas were legitimated. Reform opinion was solicited and debated within the administration. The ideology advocated twenty years earlier during the Mitchel administration was put into practice.

Mayor LaGuardia was intent on building a virtuous as well as an efficient civil service that would serve as a model for his administration. He wanted college graduates in the administration in order to give the civil service some "class." This idea had first been suggested in the Bruère report to Mayor John Mitchel, and LaGuardia was the first to put it into practice. As reported by William Brown, in an unpublished Ph.D. dissertation on LaGuardia written in 1960,

the Mayor believed strongly in a "scientific" approach to government. It was not the "science" of administrative experts that LaGuardia had in mind but rather an intense interest in the "gadgets" and details. He was in favor of testing, civil service, new and more efficient lights, better police cars, consolidated county offices, but he was interested in them as specifics rather than as issues resulting from any ordered philosophy.[16]

Bureau chiefs under LaGuardia instituted a course at New York University entitled "Government and Administration in New York City." With the tuition from the course, a scholarship for civil servants who wished to study at City College was established. And, in 1939, the division of public services training was founded at the college. The *Public Personnel Quarterly,* a digest of personnel information and research in the civil service, was first published during LaGuardia's administration.

LaGuardia is important to the current study because he was the first mayor to use civil servants as bureau chiefs. In 1936, he wanted to appoint Joseph Goodman, a career civil servant, as commissioner of water supply, gas, and electricity. Since such an appointment was prohibited by law, the mayor decided to circumvent the law and create the post of administrative assistant in every department. The appointment of Mr. Goodman marked the beginning of a senior civil service system in New York City.

The charter revisions of 1933 also helped LaGuardia. The charter was not exactly what LaGuardia wanted nor did he need it to gain control of the bureaucracy's fast development under his tenure. The expense budget, however, and not the capital budget, would prove to be the undoing of this mayor's powers. For the charter reconstituted the City Council as a part-time legislature with proportional representation, while abolishing the Board of Aldermen. The Board of Estimate was granted control over the capital budget for all boroughs. The revisions also created a six-member planning commission to monitor capital expenditures and projects. The planning commission had to approve a project before the Board of Estimate would authorize expenditures for it. The position of deputy mayor was also created in this charter.

LaGuardia's administration was a high point in the history of public service. The mayor used the momentum of the New Deal, the instability of Tammany leadership, and the renewed enthusiasm of academic reformers to impose new standards on the city's civil service.

The city's fiscal crisis during the depression years was used to consolidate municipal powers in a way not seen since the days of Boss Tweed. LaGuardia unified the subway system by purchasing the near-bankrupt Brooklyn-Manhattan Transit (BMT) and Interborough Rapid Transit (IRT) systems. These purchases increased the number of public jobs, as did Moses' plans for building parks and bridges. LaGuardia added even more jobs by reforming every city department. The 1936 charter, written by such reformers as Adolph A. Berle, replaced the Board of Aldermen with a city council and introduced proportional representation. Through this form of representation, reformers were able to reduce the power of Tammany by eliminating functional county government (i.e., reducing the administrative responsibilities of the borough presidents). But the most important victory for the academic reformers was the creation of the city planning commission. In this committal to planning, the Taylorites' dream had come true.

LaGuardia was a hard-working, enthusiastic mayor and a highly visible executive, making surprise visits to departments and personally directing his subordinates. Despite these qualities, he was not without his detractors, who viewed his use of administrative chauvinism as a means of building a reputation as a tough politician. Brown also noted the mayor's predilection for histrionics and characterized him as almost continuously "On Stage."[17]

Rexford G. Tugwell, terming LaGuardia "the little giant . . . in danger of becoming a clucking busybody," has explained that

it was . . . partly because he was an uncertain administrator that LaGuardia become dictatorial. . . . Good administrators know how to sort out the more important from the less important decisions, how to find effective subordinates and charge them with responsibilities, how to follow their performance without interfering. LaGuardia knew none of this and never found any of it out.[18]

Despite these flaws, Mayor LaGuardia made a profound impact on the development of the city civil service system. He gave it exposure and credibility among college-educated New Yorkers, and his performance has yet to be matched by any other mayor.

RESEARCH AND MAYORAL EMPOWERMENT

In 1946 William O'Dwyer, with the help of Tammany, was elected mayor. O'Dwyer wanted to introduce management-control techniques into the municipal civil service. He did little toward this end, but he did establish a body called the Mayor's Committee on Management Survey. Lazarus Joseph, the city comptroller, was made chairman, and Luther Gulick, a pioneer in the study of public administration, was appointed executive director.

The committee spent $2.2 million and produced a long report entitled "Modern Management for the City of New York." The report, a litany of academic reform proposals, recommended the creation of an office of Director of Administration. The new post, which was first advocated during the Mitchel administration, would free the mayor from administrative details. The then-governor, Thomas Dewey, also started to look more closely at the possibility of city reorganization by creating the Temporary State Commission to study the organization and structure of the city of New York. Dewey named Devereux C. Josephs, a businessman, to head the commission, but the real staff work was done by ex-civil service commissioner and political scientist Wallace Sayre. Initially, this was to have been a comprehensive investigation into the feasibility of a city-manager form of local government, but the report made recommendations similar to those of the Gulick committee. The Josephs' commission called this new administrative post the Office of City Administrator.[19]

During the administration of Mayor Vincent R. Impellitteri (1950–1954), several reports were generated by the Mayor's Committee on Management Survey. This group was a blue-ribbon commission, with a relatively large staff, nine subcommittees, and an army of consultants. It produced a comprehensive study of city administration. Griffenhagen and Associates, a private consulting agency, conducted an elaborate study of the city's personnel classification and pay policy. The agency recommended elimination of 86,000 of the 225,000 positions in the city service, a plan for classifying 1,000 vocational categories and occupations, and the establishment of a new compensation plan with twenty-seven pay scales.

Joseph Schechter, then council to the New York State Department of Civil Service, conducted a study that dealt with the city's pension policy. At that time, the city was spending 17 percent, or $132 million, of its revenues on pensions. Schechter was critical of the city's retirement system, calling it "an extensive patchwork of interwoven but mutually oblivious provisions of law." This report advocated the merger of the city employee and the Board of Education retirement systems, and noted the need for a complete revamping of the pension system.

In 1954, Richardson, Bellows, Henry, and Company, Inc.—another private consulting agency—in reviewing the recruitment and examination practices of the city, found the Municipal Civil Service Commission underfinanced, understaffed, and generally ill equipped to function properly in the area of personnel administration. The agency recommended new examinations, repeal of the "Lyons law" (a 1937 city residency law), and a general upgrading of salaries to make them competitive with those in the private sector.

The Bureau of the Budget also proposed a reorganization of the municipal Civil Service Commission. The commission would be replaced by a department of civil service, to be headed by a personnel administrator who would perform the day-to-day activities of the department. The personnel administrator would be selected by competitive examination and would not be a member of the new commission. Aside from performing the traditional functions of the Civil Service Commission, the new department would maintain a research and training division and a personnel council, which would act as a liaison to the operating departments.

In a separate study, Professors Wallace Sayre and Herbert Kaufman endorsed the Griffenhagen proposal of incentive pay together with a standard compensation-classification system. They recommended that the city create a personnel advisory board, a municipal council, and a labor-relations bureau. These new agencies would provide professional assistance to the mayor's office. They also recommended that the city develop a close relationship with universities for the recruitment of city managers. To the surprise of many, Sayre and Kaufman also recommended that the Civil Service Commission be abolished.[20]

Of all the reports, the Sayre and Kaufman studies brought the most acrimonious responses from the civil service commissioners. The commissioners asserted that the Sayre-Kaufman report was not a serious scientific study, but a "piece of propaganda." The commissioners were particularly angry with Professor Kaufman:

What disturbed the Commission particularly in connection with this report is the caliber of the "experts" whom Dr. Gulick has employed to tell the city how it should run its business. The Commission can find nothing noteworthy in the record of Dr. Kaufman in the field of public personnel administration. With respect to Dr. Sayre, there is a record of failure as Civil Service Commissioner of the City of New York. During his regime, public confidence in the merit system fell to its lowest level.[21]

These exchanges were a part of a general debate about the conduct of employee relations and also reflected the growing rift between academic reformers and politicians. Nonetheless, elected officials had grown accustomed to the civil service commission as a grand patronage resource. Hence, they refused to abolish it. The disaffection between reformers and politicians, exemplified by these reports, created an opportunity for a new type of alliance between politicians and em-ployee organization leaders.

MAYORAL POWER AND THE NEW ALLIANCE

Robert Wagner began his term of office as mayor by totally restructur-ing the civil service. With minor modifications, he implemented recom-mendations made by the Mayor's Committee on Management. Wagner placed the municipal Civil Service Commission under the wing of the personnel director. This represented a major shift in emphasis in personnel recruitments. The new director was the mayor's man, not the commission's. If the 1883 civil service law was a triumph for the genteel reformers, and the Mitchel administration for middle-class reform in general, then the Wagner years can be considered the years of revenge for civil servants. Wagner proved to be most accommodating to the aspirations of public employees. This reputation allowed him to transform the Civil Service Commission personnel department into an arm of the mayor's office called the City Department of Personnel.

ACADEMIC REFORMERS AND THE NEW ALLIANCE

John V. Lindsay, a liberal Republican, came to office as a reform mayor. Lindsay's Policy Planning Council was a type of oversight committee which helped the mayor set priorities. Although the council had the mayor's support, it never became a form of cabinet administration. Lindsay appointed Harold Riegelman, a former Wagner appointee, as chairman of a task force to look into the New York City personnel system; this was to be a two-year study of the civil service. Lindsay, a critic of the civil service, advocated strict mayoral control over all executive positions. He also wanted to attract leading urban specialists to the top jobs in city government.

Serving as mayor during the time of the civil rights movement, Lindsay was pressured into dropping the high school diploma requirement for some civil service positions. This reduction of minimum-education requirements allowed more blacks and Puerto Ricans to enter the civil service system. The mayor began to set up new job titles for the poor, and many positions created during Lindsay's "war on poverty" were made permanent.

It was during the Lindsay administration that the crystallization of the higher civil service jobs in the Managerial Pay Plan occurred. High-ranking civil servants were given a special and separate pay category. In creating the plan the mayor became the first chief executive to ascribe status to civil service managers. This group was now recognized as having policy responsibility and was separated from the regular civil service. During the Lindsay administration the public employee reached new political heights. Many union leaders were anti-Lindsay, and as a result, Lindsay went out of his way to appease them and to solicit their support for re-election. In 1969, when he lost his bid for the Republican nomination for a second term, he ran as a Liberal and won the election anyway. He subsequently left the Republican party, during his second term as mayor, and became a Democrat.

Lindsay was extremely concerned about management and tried to increase his control over a growing bureaucracy by creating superagencies out of the various independent fiefdomlike departments. Reorganization was not new to New York City, but Lindsay's plan was significant in terms of its scope. The mayor's plan succeeded in reorganizing many departments into superagencies. The new "administrations" were designed to coordinate related functions of government and make them more efficient.

Under the Lindsay reorganization plan, the departments of personnel, city planning, law and corporation counsel, and investigation remained the same, but most of the bureau and other departments of the city were restructured into superagencies or *administrations*. The new administrations were economic development, environmental protection, finance, health services, housing and development, municipal services, parks, recreation and cultural affairs, and transportation.

The reorganization of the bureaus and departments into *administrations* was a bold move toward department-centered government. Each administrator would be responsible for the department commissioners within his administrative cluster. For example, the environmental protection administrator was responsible for the Department of Air Resources, Sanitation, and Water Resources. The Lindsay plan called for strong administrators with national reputations in their fields. It thereby created a situation that divided city managers into nationals and locals. Locals—i.e., persons recruited vertically from the civil service—were used primarily as bureau chiefs and department commissioners. Bureaus and departments fought to retain their identity and independence. The sanitation and the cultural affairs departments resisted being under the aegis of an administration and reporting to an administrator. The friction between the old-line administration and the Lindsay team created a tossed-salad situation. Each group fought to make its presence felt without losing its identity. The mixing was a poor one and left a legacy of hostility.

Bureaucrats received the reorganization with mixed feelings. Two recently completed studies of the reorganized departments raise many doubts about the extent to which the individual agencies have allowed themselves to be integrated within these superagencies.* Bureaucrats fight reorganization because it throws the internal politics of agencies into

---

*See Carl Roy Schneider, "Implementing Mayor Lindsay's Reorganization: A Political Analysis of Administrative Reform in Human Resources Administration," (New York: Ph.D. diss., Columbia University, 1976) and Ronald L. Reisner, "The Politics of Municipal Reorganization: A Case study of the Political History of New York City Transportation Department," (New York: Ph.D. diss., Columbia University, 1977).

turmoil. Many city agencies continue to operate today in the manner described by Sayre and Kaufman in their 1960 book, *Governing New York City*.

FISCAL PROBLEMS AND MAYORALTY CONTROLS

The 1973 election of Abraham Beame was seen as a backlash against the reform administration of John Lindsay. In his campaign, Beame promised to return New York to sound fiscal management. Two years into his mayoralty, however, the city experienced its worst fiscal crisis since the Great Depression. The result was that his remaining years in office were spent answering questions, explaining fiscal inconsistencies, and working on budget packages in order to meet the city's mounting debts. The political implications of the Beame administration are discussed in Chapter 5; for the present, it is sufficient to note that Beame did not make a discerning impact on personnel management or employee relations. Although he succeeded in dismantling some superagencies inherited from the Lindsay administration, he did not have any alternative management system for the city, nor did his appointment of three personnel directors represent an attempt to forge a new strategy for city workers.

Near the end of the Beame years, it was announced that the city personnel office would use "broad-banding," or the practice of reducing titles by collapsing them into large categories, as a means of improving the productivity and mobility of city workers. But the largest city union, District 37, immediately labeled the idea of a lump-salary group as inflationary. Victor Gotbaum, head of the union, asserted that the price for this would be increased responsibilities. In any case, broad-banding is a "tidying-up" tactic rather than a serious change in the power relations among the various interest groups. In summary, the personnel office under Mayor Beame spent most of its time managing attrition rates, terminations, and defending itself against those who wanted its powers reduced. The charter revision of 1975, however, was adopted, and the Personnel Department underwent several structural changes.

CHARTER REVISION, PERSONNEL ADMINISTRATION, AND LABOR RELATIONS

The charter revision of 1975 represented a significant change in mayoralty powers, but not necessarily one in the politics of city-employee relations. The new charter, originally hailed as a model of municipal reform, was actually not very innovative. Yet a careful examination of its provisions is necessary in order to understand how they have affected personnel-relations administration.

Aside from being the first charter revision since 1901 to reduce the mayor's power over the budget, the 1975 charter denied the mayor a vote on the Board of Estimate, which has oversight over the capital budget. This change therefore reduced the mayor's leverage in formulating the capital budget. Also, the provision allowing the Board of Estimate and the City Council to veto a budget proposal by a two-thirds vote means additional loss of strength for the mayor. These changes in mayoralty budget power reallocated influence and responsibility. Theoretically speaking, the roles of the City Council and of the borough presidents regarding the budget were enlarged. This granting of more legislative power to the borough presidents may have created more borough rivalry, however.

The 1975 charter increased the powers of each Community Planning Board to set spending priorities and evaluate services within the five boroughs. These fifty-member boards, appointed by the borough presidents, have been a new source of patronage and political strength for local politicians. Twenty-five members are appointed by the borough president and the remainder upon the recommendation of the City Council.

The charter revision also reduced the authority of the city's Personnel Department with regard to the conduct of employee relations by placing the department on coequal status with the operating agencies. This was done by undercutting the freedom of the Personnel Department to negotiate with other agencies.

The following are the seven specific changes made in the personnel system: [22]

1. The personnel director shall assume the administrative duties and rule-making authority of the Civil Service Commission to eliminate divided responsibility for personnel administration.

This language suggests that the academic reformers had finally toppled the last remaining symbol (i.e., the Civil Service Commission) of the era of genteel reform. Actually the provision simply formalized a long-standing practice in which the personnel director had dominated the Civil Service Commission since the time of the Wagner administration. It did, however, remove the potential influence of lay commissioners in the conduct of personnel administration, a point the genteel reformers thought essential to a merit system in a democratic society.

2. Agency heads shall be responsible for personnel management functions essential for efficient agency operations in the areas of position allocation, recruitment, evaluation of qualifications, conduct of promotion examinations, incentive programs, training, performance evaluation and equal opportunity programs. Agency plans for the assumption of personnel functions shall be approved by the mayor, monitored by the personnel director and withdrawn for abuse. The Personnel Department shall promulgate standards and guidelines for delegated functions, post-audit compliance and be empowered to reverse specific agency actions based on a finding of abuse.[23]

Politicians have traditionally lamented at not being able to hire their cronies soon after an election. Boss Tweed was not the first to inveigh against red tape in hiring or to covet more authority in the recruitment process. The quoted provision has not really given them that power, however, and it may not have even materially changed the relative bargaining strengths of the personnel office or the operating agencies.

Eliminating the language that included the Civil Service Commission did not contradict the basic intent of the reformers. Ultimately the provision increased the power of the individual agent or department personnel official while eroding the initiative of the department as a whole. In their efforts to reduce personnel department power, the reformers unwittingly created multiple showdown opportunities. (Chapter 6 discusses ways in which personnel officials can demonstrate their value to the individual operating agencies.) The confrontation between the Consumer Affairs Department and the Department of Personnel shows how effective a single individual can be, even in the face of a popular commissioner armed by a majority mandate.

The most important change resulting from the charter revision was reorganization of such personnel functions as the examination, recruiting, and training bureaus. These personnel functions were grouped into task forces. There are now task forces on criminal justice (i.e., the police, district attorney, and investigation); urban affairs (human service department and boards of education); environmental protection (sanitation and air-pollution control); general government services (overhead agencies, bureau of the budget); and central control.

3. All provisional appointments shall be reviewed by the personnel department within sixty days to ensure compliance with the civil service law and all rules and regulations.

This charter change represented an effort to appease the unions and their members. During the fiscal crisis, there was much criticism of the city's retention of provisional employees (i.e., persons hired in noncompetitive categories and usually for temporary assignments). Union leaders believed that in a fiscal crisis provisional employees should be laid off before the merit-selected civil servants. The city politicians did release some provisionals, but were unwilling to remove members of the management staff who were in that category.

Most provisionals have little trouble meeting civil service requirements. Generally, provisionals are the most educated, most mobile, and most resourceful members of the city-management corps. Besides, the present system of grand patronage rarely dips into the pool of nonprofessional jobs because it does not rely on these jobs. At best, the new law simply sped up an unnecessary approval process.

4. A city-wide management service shall be established for all agencies pursuant to a plan prepared by the personnel director and approved by the mayor.

This section was designed to give the senior civil servants the recognition they deserved. The idea of a well-trained elite management staff had been advocated by academic reformers for a long time, although they had been largely unable to convince politicians of the need for a permament senior civil service. The Mitchel administration failed with its "expert-manager" scheme. The Lindsay "whiz kids" and the Managerial Pay Plan did raise the status of middle management, however. At the beginning of Mayor Beame's term, Deputy Mayor James Cavanaugh was instrumental in establishing the so-called Urban Academy at the City University of New York (CUNY) for the training of city managers, but the project was never integrated into the university structure.

In 1977 the Urban Academy reconstituted itself as a nonprofit organization and left the CUNY campus. It now provides in-service training, for a fee, for city managers. The attempt to institutionalize elitism in the city-management corps failed because civil service managers were not interested in training for training's sake. There was and is simply no enthusiasm for maintaining a high degree of professionalism. Although feelings of status deprivation are present among middle managers,[24] many managers do not see professionalism as a solution to their problems. The Managerial Employee Association (MEA) does not enjoy the full support of city managers; neither are most high-ranking civil servants members of the American Society for Public Administration (ASPA) or participants in local ASPA chapter activities. Rather than professionalism, increased salaries are the single improvement identified by most middle managers as a way to attract and retain good managers. Thus, the system of vertical recruitment and organizational insularity fosters a low level of interest in outside professional activity.

The new citywide management service may survive in name only. It may be successful in providing management internships for recent master of public administration graduates. Its future, however, as a means to elevate civil service management is uncertain for the following reasons:

First, there is no provision that requires all supervisors to be members of the management-service structure. At present, most supervisors are represented by a collective-bargaining agency. There are many advantages (i.e., higher pay and overtime) for supervisors under this arrangement. It is unlikely that the unions would allow conscription of supervisors and lose their symbiotic relationship with this group.

Second, the prospects for raising the morale of middle management were dimmed because of the fiscal crisis. Self-estrangement and status deprivation are serious problems for the individual managers, but city politics and financial conditions may preclude any real action for managers as a group. Also, the city does not have the time to conduct the job inventories and organizational climate studies necessary for the improvement of morale. It is cheaper to give the managers occasional raises.

Third, the new management service has not solved the manager retention problem of the city administration. The ambitious, capable, creative, and aggressive middle-management recruits usually get bored with the slow pace of the city administration and the seemingly arcane sponsorship system of promotion. Other young managers burn themselves out fighting the inertia of the city's highly politicized management system. Many of the best city recruits leave within two or three years for jobs in the federal government, private industry, or universities. Those who stay are less adventurous, creative, and capable. They are more likely to be looking for a permanent job, a way to stay in New York City, or a good yearly pension.

5. The Bureau of the Budget shall be removed from certification of positions to eliminate red tape and unnecessary duplication with the Personnel Department.

This provision represented a very sensible change in the recruitment process. Nevertheless, it is doubtful whether it has eliminated the red tape. The Personnel Department has always been competent in generating its own red tape, and it should welcome the lack of competition. Some of the questions raised by this provision include the following: Does the mayor's Office of Municipal Labor Relations duplicate the work of the personnel office? Who serves as fiscal watchdog of the personnel policies of the operating agencies? How will the role of the Bureau of the Budget change? A personnel department trying to plan without the involvement of the Bureau of the Budget will be an interesting development to watch.

6. The one-in-three rule for the appointment of persons from eligible lists shall be reinstated in accordance with the State Civil Service Law.

The one-in-three rule, temporarily suspended during the Beame administration and a rule insisted upon by some unionists, was thus restored. Employers are now free to select any one of the three highest scorers on the examinations. Yet it is not clear who benefits from this rule. Employers have rarely been denied their choice of applicants. As Professors Savas and Ginsburg have pointed out, the personnel department could delay an appointment until a new or outside applicant loses interest or accepts another job.[25] This rule change supported the sponsorship system of promotion, which is discussed in Chapter 6, by allowing the employer more flexibility in selecting applicants.

7. The Civil Service Commission, increased to five members appointed by the mayor, shall determine appeals of aggrieved employees and monitor the personnel administration of the city.

This last rule change appears to be a contradiction of Section 1. Why expand the commission's membership if their influence is going to be reduced? Grievance procedures are now included in union contracts. As Chapter 2 suggested, the growth possibilities for grand patronage are limited unless the mayor can effectively increase the numbers of appointments available to him. The 1975 charter allows the mayor to appoint five part-time commissioners, with a salary of more than $30,000 each, supposedly for the protection of so-called aggrieved employees. In the past, the unions had certainly demonstrated that they could adequately defend their "aggrieved members." In other words, the job of the commissioners is superfluous.

If the charter revision would only have dubious impact on the personnel policy of the city, why invest all the time and energy in a charter revision referendum? A possible explanation is the personalities of the charter commission members. New York State Senator Roy Goodman, the chairman of the Charter Revision Commission and a former Lindsay administration official, expressed his frustration about the city personnel policy at a public forum on the charter revision. He lamented the fact that his efforts to hire new people in the Department of Finance were being repeatedly thwarted by the Personnel Department. His voice barely concealed his anger and disgust at the Department of Personnel. Thus, many of the changes in personnel policies can be thought of as "Goodman's Revenge."[26] Fortunately for the senator he lost the 1976 mayoralty election, thus sparing him the task of having to implement the charter.

THE KOCH YEARS

In 1976, Edward I. Koch, a liberal reformer and congressman from the East Side of Manhattan defeated the incumbent, Mayor Beame, and five other contenders in the Democratic primary. In the general election, Republican Roy Goodman turned out to be a lackluster candidate, and Koch won handily. The campaign centered on the fiscal crisis, on Beame's alleged mishandling of city finances, and on inept city management. Koch promised to appoint only highly trained subordinates to his staff.

The transition from Beame to Koch started shortly after the primary, and took up most of Koch's first year as mayor. Nevertheless, the new municipal team successfully negotiated a loan guarantee with congressional committees, and secured federal backing for city bonds.

Soon after Koch took office, he began a highly publicized policy of dismissing, demoting, and disciplining city workers. As Thomas Roche, the city personnel director, announced:

In line with Mayor Koch's policy, I fully expect to see more cases in coming months in which the penalty is more severe than a slap on the wrist for the offending employee. We're going to be firm now. This is only to insure that city employees give a fair day's work for a fair day's pay.[27]

This policy was designed to convince the public that something was finally being done about incompetent, lazy, and absentee workers. The policy must of necessity be more symbolic than real, however, because to monitor all civil servants is impossible. Professor Murray Edelman has observed that "concrete legal objectives are ordinarily pursued as though administrators and potential defiers were involved in a game rather than with clear rule. The basic rule is that a fairly large proportion of the instances of compliance will not be detected or penalized."[28]

The potential defiers accept the fact that they are playing a game, and they may also be willing to pay when they get caught in the act. It is a matter of calculating the risk when a policeman decides to go to sleep in his patrol car, when park workers sell flowers to the public, or when sanitation workers on the night shift have a few rounds of beer at the local bar. Edelman also has stated that

where enforcement is played as a game, none of those involved pretends that the offense is virtuous; but all recognize, through mutual role-taking, that there are temptations, that there is a shared interest in resisting them; and that, within the rules, offenders caught under specified conditions shall pay the specified penalties.[29]

Aside from the problems of enforcement, a civil servant will not necessarily be deterred by the public dismissal of a colleague. Absenteeism, corruption, and laziness will continue in spite of highly publicized dismissals. Such publicized dismissals are very much akin to the eighteenth-century English policy of publicly hanging pickpockets—a practice that unfortunately did not end pickpocketing, some pockets even being picked during the course of the hangings.

Koch has advocated the passage of a residency law, as he promised to do during his campaign. Once in office, the mayor found many supporters for this law because of a 1976 United States Supreme Court decision, *McCarty* v. *Philadelphia,* which upheld Philadelphia's residency law. In July 1978, the New York City Council passed Local Law No. 20, which required city employees to live within city limits. The Board of Education followed with a regulation stipulating that newly hired teachers must reside in the city. Although these laws were not retroactive, they caused considerable debate and nurtured court challenges. Unions also were opposed to the laws despite the fact that only a minority (20 percent) of their members lived outside the city. Victor Gotbaum argued, "I just don't believe that groups of people ought to be told where to live because of where they work. It is a civil rights issue. You can't have second-class citizens."[30]

Although the Supreme Court dismissed the Gotbaum argument, many people still believe that such a requirement constitutes a question of civil liberties. Koch's defense of the residency law rests on the assumption and assertion that living within the city portrays and perpetuates a psychological commitment to the city and its problems: "If you're a fireman you're much more concerned if *your* home is burning. If you are a policeman, you are much more concerned if *your* family is under attack. If you're a sanitation man, you're much more concerned if *your* street is dirty."[31] Koch and the law's supporters also argue that such a law will help to reduce the flight of dollars and residents to the suburbs. These arguments, however persuasive, were not enough for New York State Supreme Court Justice Sidney Asch, who overruled Local Law No. 20.[32] This happened because residency laws are under the jurisdiction of the state legislature only, and no city council can pass a law that takes precedence over state law. In addition, the state legislature has not yet changed its laws to allow this kind of municipal action, having taken the position that

the history of residency laws suggests that employees resent them and seek to circumvent enforcement. Unions regard them as an issue of negotiation and will insist upon a role in writing such laws. Unions can fight such laws in the state legislature where they will have the support of the suburban legislators. Despite the Court ruling, the prospects for a proliferation of residency laws are dim.[33]

The New York State Legislature continues to thwart the personnel activism of Mayor Koch. Despite his objections, it passed the so-called Heart bill, which allows firemen to retire with three-quarters pay if they develop a heart ailment during city employment, whether on or off the job. The mayor's response to this act was, "It broke my heart."[34] This defeat along with that of general civil service reform demonstrates how interest groups can block a mayor, and unless or until Koch recognizes the role of the state legislature as the last "court of appeals" for interest groups, it seems likely that he will continue to have his policy reversed, overruled, and amended.

In addition to the earlier changes wrought in 1975, in the city charter, Koch also moved to make revisions in the personnel system through the charter. His legislative effort represented a bold move for the new mayor. He asked the state legislature to pass a law that would prohibit supervisors from belonging to the same union as their subordinates. Among other things, he advocated three-year appointments for managerial personnel, the expansion of exempt classes, a new one-in-ten rule (i.e., allowing recruiters ten applicant choices rather than the present three), authority to transfer personnel without their consent, and the assignment of more quantitative weight for performance evaluation than for seniority in layoff decisions. Koch would also give all new starting employees the same equal seniority. The Koch reform called for the expansion of city control over all municipal employees, consolidation of bargaining units, and a no-bargaining clause for management rights.

These reforms were sweeping in nature and met enormous resistance in the personnel area. The unions were able to defeat the reforms in the state legislature. For the first time, the public employees' union showed unexpected strength in the Republican-controlled state senate. Other members of the personnel system also expressed reservations about the Koch reforms. Citizens Union issued its own protest with regard to the civil service reforms. It argued that the Management Service Plan mandated by the charter revision should be given priority in city government. Citizens Union advocated an inventory of managerial skills among present employees: more training, better performance appraisals, the end of restrictions in the selection process (i.e., one in three), the development of middle management, and a general reduction in the definition of managerial titles.

Citizens Union ended its critique by demanding a provision that would have the mayor provide leadership in the implementation of the Management Service Plan. The proposal concluded:

In the past many widely procedural reforms in City government, particularly in personnel administration, have ultimately produced no substantive change. The reform impulse that generated them has been smothered in the routines of the personnel system, and the innovative goals have been ignored by a business-as-usual bureaucracy. The Management Service Plan can easily become another link in this sorry chain of opportunities lost. Only through firm leadership at the top can the promise of better management which the Plan offers to New York City be realized.[35]

Citizens Union also issued a strong endorsement of the principle of public-impact statements on union contract terms and agreements. It claimed that the public had a right to know about any negotiations between the unions and the city. The press has also traditionally advocated more public access to city records. Although the press endorsed civil service reform, it alone was unable to rally enough enthusiasm for a legislative struggle. The debate over the Koch municipal reform turned out to be one of the most low-key affairs in personnel conflicts. After all the provisions had been seriously amended by friendly interest groups and vetoed by the unions, Koch found that he did not have many supporters in the state legislature for his proposal, so he withdrew the package.

SUMMARY

The quest for mayoral control of city personnel policy has not been without the illusion of victory, the certainty of defeat—neither of which has served to quell the ambitions of newly elected mayors. The pursuit of executive-centered government continues as department-centered employees become more skilled at protecting their own interests.

Reformers now advocate a single personnel director who works directly for the mayor. This trend toward more centralization of authority is a reversal of the reformist position in the early nineteenth century. In effect, academic reformers, consciously or unconsciously, have contributed to the underutilization of the urban legislature (i.e., the City Council) in personnel policy.

Three other themes emerge from this view of New York City's personnel politics since the turn of the century. First, group dynamics have consistently undermined the technical structure of a recruiting system based on merit. A system based purely on merit has remained a distant goal in personnel policy. Because the political arena offers swift and reliable results, most veteran interest-group leaders have abandoned merit as a working principle. Nevertheless, new interest groups use the term "merit" to justify and legitimize their claims and position in the personnel field. Every group, including the reformers, has relaxed its standards of merit when its candidate's position was at stake. Second, interest-group leaders exploit public-policy issues for political ends. Rarely are these issues examined in depth, either by the affected group or by the press. Because of the media's demands that politicians and bureaucrats go on record about issues, they have often resorted to dramaturgy in order to appear competent. This results in a cursory analysis of serious public issues by all those involved. Third and finally, the management of the city administration has always been more political than technical. Therefore most changes for the better are determined by group politics rather than by any technical breakthrough.

Mayor Koch, like his idol, Mayor LaGuardia, has personalized the mayoralty. He has encouraged the notion that he is an independent, "a tell-it-like-it-is," outspoken person. This verbally aggressive campaign has resulted in a shift of attention to the mayor and to the city's minority groups.

A "Lone Ranger" approach to politics is good theater but can cause problems for a mayor in the personnel area. As emphasized in the previous chapter, the municipal-employee field is not amenable to individual action. A single person may draw attention to problems, but he or she will almost surely find it difficult to make major changes in the personnel system alone.

Mayor Koch's decision to push for reform seems to have been ill timed and counter to the rules of the personnel community. This is not to gainsay efficacy of personality, character, and style, however, in the exercise of mayoralty power. George McClellan, a Tammany-elected mayor seized the initiative and instituted needed reforms in the city civil service system. Even such a Kafkaesque figure as William Gaynor was able to ignore patronage demands from Tammany and to publicize his reforms, and the colorful Fiorello LaGuardia proved to be a strong mayor; even before the passage of the 1938 charter revisions, the Great Depression enabled him to make changes in the civil service system. For aggressive mayors, theatricality has apparently proved to be more effective in achieving administrative objectives than charter revision.

4

UNIONS AS INTEREST GROUPS
IN PERSONNEL POLICY

Before the fiscal crisis of 1975, the New York City theater of angry workers was one of the most exciting shows in town. Public employees and union leaders were the true celebrities of city politics. New York City seemed to be a union town; it enjoyed the most colorful and articulate group of union leaders in the nation. These men could turn a phrase, make a threat, or debate anyone at anytime. The fiscal crisis may have dampened their spirits, but they still retain today a very respectable position in city politics.

Labor leaders view themselves as brokers. Brokers are agents or middlemen who represent sellers or products. They are authorized by the sellers to negotiate prices and deliver agreements. The higher the price that a broker obtains, the more he or she is seen as competent and tough by those selling. The sellers in this case are the city workers, and the product is their labor. Selling labor is a most difficult task, one that requires the finest thespian skills. The typical municipal labor leader has to sell his product to the city, the negotiated agreement to the membership, and the salary increments to the public.

Civil servants as members of a collective-bargaining organization are a difficult group to please. Many have come to believe that they are the supplicants of partisan politics and the targets of taxpayers' frustrations. For them, espirit de corps is difficult to come by, and any seller of such a dream must be able to produce the bottom line—money and mobility. Municipal workers want the salaries and the prestige of their private-sector counterparts. Thus unions are seen as mechanisms for change, but labor politicians are dispensable. In union elections, union members attempt to maximize their economic self-interest; they vote their utility income.

For these reasons, any labor leader must be good with the media. He or she must be able to cite statistical information without notes, to appear indignant or angry at critical moments in a media interview, and to flatter the media personality when required. Unlike the old brokers of the political machine, modern labor leaders cannot always promise that what has been obtained at the bargaining table can be sold to the membership. Dramatizing an independent membership is thus an important ploy used by labor leaders to prove that their group is a democratic organization. "I am not their boss; they are my boss" is what the modern union official will often say. Most labor leaders cite this as an improvement over the old Tammany Hall system in which discipline was rigid and workers were supplicants. Stoddard's description of the early Tammany organization is a situation most modern brokers would wish to avoid:

First and foremost, Tammany taught discipline. Tammany is a volunteer army, and strict obedience to orders is the basis of its power. As in Napoleon's armies, the rawest recruit carries a marshal's baton in his knapsack; the "career is open to talent." Yet straight and narrow is the path to advancement. Promotion comes only through a merit system, rigid as the law of Medes and Persians, which even the big Boss never breaks. And the first article of the Tammany code is that he who would lead must first serve; he who would command must know how, promptly and implicitly, to obey.[1]

The aim of the present chapter is to show how relatively less-disciplined organizations (unions) became the leading spokesmen for New York civil servants at the expense of Tammany in particular and the political parties in general. This chapter is also concerned with the institutionalization and politicization of the collective-bargaining process.

Before turning to the historical development of the municipal unions in New York City, it may be useful to refine our definition of these unions. For present purposes, employee organizations are characterized by three types: affiliates, occupational associations, and mutual-benefit societies.

Affiliates are local organizations of national unions. Theoretically they can draw on the prestige, support and political resources of the larger organization, but in New York City this assistance has rarely been needed. Modeled after the private-sector trade-union movement, these organizations attempt to impose generally accepted principles of labor relations on city departments. As a rule, the leadership of the central staff is composed of professional labor organizers; occupation titles and departments are usually organized into local units. The leadership of the local units comes from the membership. Members of the union are recruited by organizing, raiding other organizations, and conscription. As inclusive organizations, their aim is to recruit every worker in the city government. They have generally been more effective than other labor organizations because of their professional leadership, trade-unionist ideology, and political connections. Most affiliates are very involved in city politics and maintain an active legislative lobby.

Associations function much like the affiliates except that they are independent organizations. They rarely, however, recruit from outside their own occupations or departments. The Patrolmen's Benevolent Association does not recruit officers from the city's correction departments. Associations are mass-membership organizations and elect their leaders from the membership. Consequently, the internal structure of the organization is less bureaucratic, and there is a high rate of turnover in the leadership.

The members of mutual-benefit societies are usually exempted by law or occupational tradition from engaging in collective bargaining and from becoming members of labor unions. Lobbying is the principal method of generating support for the membership's goals. These organizations are also mass-membership oriented and elect their leadership from their ranks.

The orientation of an employee organization is determined by tradition, occupation, and history. Local occupation groups shop for employees that fit their status and economic interests. The political history of municipal departments reveals much about employees' organizations and their leaders.

Civil Service Unions Replace Tammany Hall. If the excesses of the Sons of Tammany gave birth to the civil-service reform movement, then party politics accelerated the development of civil service organizations. It was the municipal workers who had to pay Tammany for their jobs. The municipal workers had to vote right, and if the party lost, they often lost their jobs. Job insecurity, low pay, and poor working conditions stimulated the growth of benevolent associations. In the late eighteen eighties the labor movement was beginning to make itself felt among working-class New Yorkers. The Henry George mayoral candidacy and the Socialist movement were attempts to translate the labor movement into a political force. The history of the New York civil service might have developed differently if Henry George had won in 1886.

Henry George did not win because of a coalition of businessmen, genteel reformers, and the church, engineered by Tammany Hall's Richard Croker. The genteel reformers were opposed to employee organizations; they viewed such organizations as being another way of avoiding the merit system and protecting the jobs of incompetent and corrupt public employees. The reformers also believed that public-employee unions were inconsistent with a businesslike approach to government. This attitude was a carry-over from antilabor attitudes within the private sector. The reformers thought that all city workers should be considered as individuals and stand on their personal qualifications rather than on their membership in an organization. Labor organizations were seen by civil service reformers as inimical to the principles of the merit system.

Part of the immigrant workers' complaints against the reform administration was the expressed preference of the reformers for nonjob-related requirements at the expense of job skill and experience. The immigrants supported employee organizations, in part, as a reaction to what they viewed as the arbitrary imposition of these requirements. Immigrant artisans, for example, were required to be able to read and write English. Immigrants and Tammany politicians maintained that in the nineteenth century experience alone was sufficient to do most city jobs. In any case, the immigrants supported Tammany Hall against the reformers and in turn received the party's support in their fight against written examinations.

The reformers felt that a general level of intelligence was the most important criterion for a civil service career. Edward Shepard, one of the reformers who lobbied for the 1883 state civil service legislation, wrote the regulations for Brooklyn: "General intelligence and general force are often indeed far more important than actual experience. The value of experience in most places is enormously overrated." Shepard carried this view even further by stating that "long experience may be a sign of a low order of skill. There may be no promise of improvement."[2] Protestant reformers expressed some implicit and explicit prejudices against Catholic immigrants. Clifford W. Patton saw the immigrants as an impediment to reform:

Most of the foreigners who entered the United States in the late nineteenth century were attracted to the cities, which offered such visible advantages as employment, parks, concerns, and charities. New York City received the greatest number: in 1880, 44% of her population was foreign-born. While many immigrants were of course good and useful citizens, the majority were ignorant and credulous, unaccustomed to the privilege of the ballot, and with no conception of the true aims of municipal government. The mixture of so many nationalities, the lack of homogeneity, made the problem of city government infinitely more difficult.[3]

Patton's statement contains a typical stereotyped view of immigrants. The immigrants brought more than poverty and ignorance to America;

they brought their political ideas, such as Socialism and Syndicalism. New York City was large enough to accommodate such ideas and economically strong enough to absorb these workers. The private sector was expanding, and union organizing followed. When the private sector began to migrate to other parts of the country, organizers intensified their efforts in the public sector. A person could make a living by union organizing, and it was no accident that New York City became known as a labor-union town.

New York ranks first among the nation's cities with respect to the growth and success of public-employee unions. The political reason for this growth is the fragmented nature of its political parties. The decline of Tammany and the demise of the local Republican party-reform coalition as a viable alternative accelerated the growth of public-employee organizations. Author Wirt Howe's comment about the Republican party still holds true today:

The general opinion that I retain of the Republican party in New York City is that it was not unlike the same party in the far South, a feeble group sustained by the power of the party in Washington, accomplishing practically nothing locally and through the domination of unworthy leaders a mere foil for the Democrats and source of a more personal benefit to a few ringleaders. But with the racial, religious, and political conditions what they were in New York, it is hard to see how things could have been otherwise there or in the South either.[4]

Benevolent Societies and Associations: Old Unionism. The growth of public employee organizations was a result of the existing work force's efforts to standardize its relationship with its departments, to provide job security, and to obtain freedom from political contributions. Prior to 1890, Tammany was able to convince most of the city's workers that the organization would look out for their interests. Tammany painted the reformers as anti-immigrant and antiworking class. In this way the party was able to convince business that it could control the immigrants, and the immigrants that it could protect them from the reformers.

Tammany controlled the work force, especially the police force, and the police department in turn controlled the election procedures. This arrangement enabled Tammany to maintain electoral control of the city. After the civil service victory of 1883, Tammany's relationship with the reformers began to deteriorate. The reformers started fielding rival candidates, and with the advent of Citizens Union, they were able to challenge Tammany for political office.

Tammany fought the development of public-employee organizations because they threatened to restrict party influence in the city departments.

Because Tammany could offer these civil servants more benefits, it was in a better position to compete for the loyalty of city workers. Tammany even refused to tolerate or cooperate with apolitical mutual-benefit associations.

The reformers also eschewed employee groups. During the Strong Administration (1895–1897) Colonel Waring conducted arbitration experiments in the Street Department. These experiments were designed to settle worker disputes within the department and eliminate embryonic employee organizations. The Waring strategy achieved neither objective. Street cleaners became more militant and conducted strikes in 1888 and 1890. These early strikes were partially effective in raising salaries and reducing work loads and hours.

During the Mitchel reform administration (1914–1915), the academic reformers attempted to stem the tide of organizing workers by introducing the concept of intradepartment structures for worker disputes, following the principles of Taylorism which had always maintained that unions were unnecessary in an efficient city.

Mitchel's trouble with the police started when he introduced the so-called Goethal's bill ostensibly to induce General George W. Goethals, the builder of the Panama Canal, to become police commissioner. The bill would have abolished judicial review of the commissioner and other administrative decisions in the Police Department. It also would have made it easier to promote policemen from within the ranks. The Patrolmen's Benevolent Association responded to the bill with a letter-writing campaign and by lobbying state legislators, and thus defeated the proposed measure.

The Teamsters remained active and attempted to reorganize the street cleaners as early as 1906, but failed in their strike attempts of 1907 and 1911. Mayor Gaynor proved a tough opponent of unions. Strikes that were attempted during his administration were met with firings, strike-breaking, and arrests. Consequently, the street cleaners returned to the nonunion organization known as the Joint Council of Drivers and Sweepers. This organization made its peace with Tammany and also acted as broker for the workers with the Sanitation Department until the LaGuardia administration came to power.

The Firemen's Mutual Benefit Association—the so-called Pinkies because of its use of pink stationery—which was organized in 1893, decided to bypass Tammany and appeal directly to the state legislature. The president of the Pinkies, James D. Clifford, was dismissed for participating in partisan politics and criticizing Richard Croker; contributing to a political fund was against the city charter. The Democratic party continued its fight against such employee organizations and was able to ban the Pinkies outright in 1913.[5] A new firemen's association, the Uniformed Firemen's Association was started in 1917. This organization later became affiliated with the International Association of Firefighters.

Founded in 1894, the New York City Patrolmen's Benevolent Association (PBA) started as a mutual-benefit organization. The organization was able to develop because Tammany was busy fighting the good government groups and Dr. Charles H. Parkhurst's Citizens' Vigilance Committee. The PBA was originally started to protect policemen from Tammany and the reformers, but its basic purpose changed to lobbying for higher salaries for policemen. The fact that Patrick McGinely was able to obtain salary increases from the legislature during the PBA's first year of existence helped recruitment greatly.

With the election of the fusion ticket of 1894, the association moved quickly to defeat the Lexow bill, which sought to give the mayor the power to appoint a police board. Opposition to any sort of civilian-review board would eventually become a permanent part of PBA strategy. With the help of Boss Thomas Platt, the PBA was able to defeat this attempt to enact civilian control over the police department. Platt, the upstate Republican party boss, was eager to undermine Tammany's influence in city politics and to demonstrate that he could deliver bills in the state legislature. Platt's organization helped initiate the Lexow Investigation, a state legislature investigation of the city administration, but he was not interested in nonpartisan reform. He wanted more city patronage for the local Republican party.

The police, with their budding organization, were firmly established in the arena of electoral politics, and fought reformers and Tammany alike. They formed coalitions and supported any politician who promised them higher salaries and better work schedules. They continued to work with Tammany candidates until the McClellan administration. At this point the PBA opposed McClellan in his reelection bid, but McClellan won the election anyway. One of his first official acts was to return the police to a two-platoon system, which meant twelve instead of eight working hours for the police. The struggle for the eight-hour day was long, and was eventually won by the association during the Gaynor administration. Mayor Gaynor, although elected with the aid of Tammany Hall, turned out to be highly independent, and he did not support the 1911 PBA-Tammany Hall-backed salary bill, which was before the state legislature and which he had promised to support during the campaign.

Gaynor's break with Tammany was permanent. Now the police

organization turned away from the city government and focused its attention on Albany. Because the reformers had no coherent administrative policy for the police department, it continued to enjoy the same autonomy as it had under Tammany. The Parkhurst crime campaign of 1892 did not result in the reevaluation of the role of the police. This would be interpreted as the genteel reformers' and academic reformers' failure to institutionalize civilian control of the police.[6]

Since the nineteenth century, the traditional image of the police as honest and law-abiding authority figures has been undermined by disclosures of corruption within the department. That the police frequently supported conservative political candidates made them suspect in the poorer communities. It was this deflation of the moral authority of the police that led to the bread-and-butter politics of the PBA leadership. The internal politics and status-deprivation concerns of the PBA caused it to seek public recognition as the union with the most highly paid city workers. This, in turn, has led to political tactics in which people's fears are manipulated.

The police have used crime statistics to alternately assure and alarm the public. Crime has always been a mainstay of the American city life. The celebration of sensational crimes and the death of policemen in the line of duty have been used to expand police manpower. The PBA has also used its power to resist most administrative changes within the police department, particularly in the area of the chain of command. The union has been equally successful in obviating an effective civilian review board.

Finally, the power of the PBA is exemplified by its ability to resist the civilianization of the police department's clerical and housekeeping functions. In securing these clerical jobs and station-house duties, the union has been able to relegate relatively risk-free duties to aging policemen. Assignment to low crime communities and high morale units are now ways to reward police loyalty to the union.

The epitome of the old unionism is the Civil Service Forum. This organization was first known as the New York Service Association (1909) and later as the New York Civil Service Society (1911). The initial organization included both state and city civil servants. Uniform-wearing services were excluded from membership. Joseph J. O'Reilly, one of the founders of the organization and editor of the *Chief,* a civil service newspaper, favored a strong nonpartisan lobbying organization.

Frank Prial, a city employee in the Department of Finance, had other ideas for the organization when he took over the leadership in 1913. First he began to build a political organization, and the election of 1913 was his first opportunity to get the organization to endorse a mayoralty candidate. Although he failed, Prial did manage to get a resolution defeated in the state legislature that favored Tammany. Tammany claimed civil service support, but the election went to the fusion ticket headed by Mitchel. Prial lost his city patronage job, and took a job with the New York State Department of Labor. He continued his fight with reformers and mobilized his organization to support the civil servants in their fight with what he termed the "bumbling" Mitchel administration's version of scientific management. This, of course, delighted Tammany, and made Prial a relatively powerful political figure.

In 1914, Joseph J. O'Reilly sought to bring all public-employee organizations under a new umbrella association called the Civil Service Forum. Mitchel reacted to growing threats of public-employee politicization by establishing shop organizations called conference committees. This attempt to coopt public-employee associations failed as it had done in the Strong administration. The attempt, however, had the effect of uniting O'Reilly, Prial, the *Chief,* and the *Chief's* rival, the *Civil Service Chronicle,* another newspaper.

Mitchel and his associates succeeded in alienating most civil servants and their organizations. Tammany and William Randolph Hearst, the publisher of the *Daily Mirror* and the *New York Journal American,* needed to convince the civil servants that they should defeat the Mitchel reelection bid. Prial actually joined the Hylan administration as deputy comptroller. Later he moved to consolidate his power by endorsing the candidacy of Alfred E. Smith for governor. The governor's veto of pay raises drove the uniformed-service workers out of the forum.

Prial then succeeded in getting the forum to declare the *Chief* as the official organ of the organization. The *Chronicle* threw its support to the forum's rival, the Municipal Employees Association (MEA), which was a weak organization seeking to unite all city employees under the AFL banner. But the organization did not achieve affiliation nor did it survive the antistrike sentiment generated by the 1919 Boston police strike. With the demise of MEA, Prial emerged with a smaller Tammany-supported organization and no rivals. He became a powerful political figure of the 1920s, but he never succeeded in penetrating the inner circle of Charles Murphy, the Tammany leader. After Murphy died in 1928, the party went into a tailspin with the Walker scandal. The combination of Walker's resignation and the Great Depression set the party up for its defeat by LaGuardia. Prial tried twice for elected office himself, but failed both times. He did serve as acting comptroller. Whatever reputation the forum had had, it diminished after Prial's 1936 defeat in a primary race for president of the Board of Aldermen. Professor Sterling Spero cites other reasons for the forum's decline:

In the mid-thirties, trade union movements began to develop in the municipal services of New York and other cities as a phase of the general labor upsurge which the country was experiencing. This was the first effective challenge to the Forum's practical monopoly in New York. The result was to drive it into renewed opposition not only to labor unionism among the city employees, but to all the demands which employee unions began to make for collective bargaining, the checkoff of dues and other features of union programs. The Forum also continued the opposition which it had always shown toward educational standards for admission to the service. It even opposed granting of credit toward promotion for study after working hours at the various universities and colleges in the city.[7]

The forum never created a mass-oriented organization. It was content with its lobbying and informative function, which had been enough to create a comfortable relationship with the politicians. The forum leaders were not ready for Jerry Wurf and the new unionism, and could not compete with Wurf's new services and programs for civil servants. After the forum opposed Robert Wagner's labor policies in the 1950s, any influence it may have had in city politics was eliminated. The Wagner-Wurf alliance was to become the new electoral connection. Nevertheless, the forum was important as the major organization of the civil service during the transition period between the reforming bureaucracy and the welfare bureaucracy.

Jerry Wurf and the New Unionism. The 1950s were the years of the gladiators, and every union had to fight for itself. The civil servants were there for the organizing. Dr. Arnold Zander, leader of the American Federation of State, County and Municipal Employees (AFSCME) sent Jerry Wurf to New York City to give life to the old State, County and Municipal Employees (SCME). Wurf was an aggressive organizer, a perfect character actor, whose strategy was to organize and consolidate all civil servants' associations and to promote collective bargaining. He took his uplift message directly to the workers, since most of the minor organizations and associations were in a state of flux, their members were ripe for raiding. One of Wurf's advantages was his organization's ability to offer national affiliation to local employee associations. Many professional organizers were recruited and provided with titles and funds to increase the crop of newly unionized city employees.

District Council 37 used a union newspaper, the *Spotlight,* to create issues and capitalize on whatever grievances the civil servants already had. The District Council soon began to absorb the weaker units of other unions. In the end, it outhustled, outorganized, and outflanked all rivals. With success and growth came rivalries, power struggles, and personality clashes. In 1951 a split occurred within AFSCME that resulted in John DeLury, the then vice-president, and Barry Feinstein's taking their followers to the Teamsters. DeLury took over what is now Teamster Local 831 of the Uniformed Sanitationmen's Association, and Feinstein became president of Teamster Local 237.

Professor Ralph Jones, in his history of District Council 37 traces this split to the personalities of DeLury, Feinstein, and Jerry Wurf.[8] DeLury and Feinstein are presented by Jones as union leaders who were seeking to establish good working relations with politicians and who thought that labor objectives could be adequately achieved through lobbying. Wurf disagreed, however, and abandoned the symbiotic relationship with politicians for collective bargaining. He assumed an adversary posture toward management and politicians. According to Jones, these tactics alienated Wurf's peers in the labor movement, and led to the major split in AFSCME.

An alternative explanation maintains that the personal ambitions of DeLury, Feinstein, and Wurf led to the split. After Wurf had established hegemony as the AFSCME chief representative in New York City, DeLury and Feinstein were unwilling to play subordinate roles. The Teamster organization offered them top leadership positions and organizations. Although the split increased competition among the various affiliates, it did not cripple the labor movement.

Professor Jones concludes that Jerry Wurf was the key factor in the transformation of employee unions in the city. Other studies, such as the one by authors Richard Billing and John Greenspan, show Wurf as a so-called Young Turk, dissatisfied with the traditional methods of organizing workers.[9] Billing and Greenspan quote statements by Wurf that reveal him as a man on a crusade who understood the potential of the New York political environment and was prepared to do what was necessary to mobilize workers. Wurf used his organizational skill, as well as the influence of the *Spotlight,* to sell unionism to nonuniformed workers. Because the District Council had the power to create new locals, Wurf was able to offer power, status, and income to the organizers of such locals.

There were 55 AFSCME locals between 1951 and 1956 when the entire District Council's membership was only 5,000. Under Wurf's leadership, the council grew to 18,000 by 1959.[10] In 1975, District Council 37 had more than 100,000 members. This growth was made possible mainly through the coopting of the weaker employee organizations, and through the institutionalization of collective bargaining. In 1964, Wurf became national president of AFSCME.

The work of Wurf was continued by Victor Gotbaum, who gained a reputation as an effective labor leader during the Lindsay administration and consolidated it during that of Beame. Gotbaum and his assistant, Lillian Roberts, have been in the forefront of resolving the problem of the Health and Hospitals Corporation, the largest municipal hospital system in the world and the largest single employer of minority workers in the city. Gotbaum's union has forged a coalition with the city minority leadership over the closing of hospitals in the minority community. This coalition, along with Gotbaum's statesmanship during the 1975 fiscal crisis, has won him many admirers and supporters. Gotbaum was named man of the year by the City Club in 1978, but as he has said many times, his members judge him not for his honors but by what he can deliver.

Despite Gotbaum's leadership and the assembling of one of the best professional teams in the nation, the union today is losing members. By 1980 District Council 37 had 93,779 members and 14,459 agency shop payers (i.e., people who are not members but are required to pay a service fee). Its closest rival in numbers and influence is the American Federation of Teachers with 63,000 members. Led by Albert Shanker, the teachers' union is the largest professional group in the city.

The personalities of men like Gotbaum, Shanker, and Feinstein, along with their contract economic consultant, Jack Bigel, make them perfectly suited for media-oriented contract negotiations. Gotbaum takes a beseeching approach. He argues that anything can be negotiated. Shanker can be tough, but usually takes the "high ground" which exemplifies his teacher constituency. He perpetuates the image of a tough labor leader whose primary concern is the quality of the schools.

Barry Feinstein once had charges brought against him for allowing his workers to leave the city's drawbridges open. This 1960 traffic-paralyzing tactic won him a reputation as a supermilitant. In the early eighties he has emerged as a moderate advocate for his union.

The late John DeLury had a reputation for militant and Machiavellian tactics. He skillfully used the strike threat throughout his career. Visions of garbage-laden streets always lurked in the minds of New Yorkers. DeLury was also skilled at coopting city sanitation commissioners regardless of social background or political views. During the Lindsay administration, he attacked the mayor but praised his sanitation commissioner, in effect creating obligations among the city's commissioners while retaining his reputation as a militant.

Of all the union notables Jack Bigel, the consultant, is the most interesting. During the 1975 fiscal crisis he seemed to take delight in second-guessing the fiscal managers sent by the investment community to straighten out the city's finances. He always manages to sound more authoritative than the opposing expert.

Because of their long tenures in office, all these leaders have developed a good working relationship with the media. Many unions change their leadership at more frequent intervals. The police, fire, and corrections unions, for instance, rarely elect presidents for more than one term. The unintended consequences of the mass-membership orientation is that leaders are at a disadvantage with the media because they are not allowed sufficient time to make friends with reporters, reformers, and city officials.

Strikes and Antistrike Laws. The strike continues to be the most controversial action taken by public employees. Although striking public employees are as American as apple pie, some individuals still have trouble digesting the notion of public employees exercising this right. In 1941 Professors Sterling Spero, Eliot Kaplan, and Arthur Macmahon debated the legitimacy of strikes among public employees. Kaplan opposed the right to strike for public employees, but Spero and Macmahon took a more accommodating view.[11] For them the issue needed to be analyzed in terms of the growing numbers of public employees and the expansion of government services.

The opposition to public employees' strikes surfaced again in the works of Harry H. Wellington and Ralph K. Winter and that of David Stanley and Carole Cooper.[12] Nonetheless public employees continue to support the use of the strike weapon as a facilitating device for collective bargaining.

Clearly the willingness to strike and to engage in collective bargaining separates the new unionism from the old. The old unionists used lobbying and the legislative process to secure higher wages, better fringe benefits, and favorable working conditions. The early public-employee organizations agreed with the reformers that strikes were inappropriate for public employees. The public employees did attempt strikes, but these either failed or else served to alienate the public. The negative outcome of the Boston police strike of 1919 undermined the concept of the strike as a tactic for negotiation. AFSCME was officially against strikes in the 1930s and 1940s.

New York State was a pioneer in antistrike legislation. Reacting to the successful Buffalo teachers' strike of 1947, the state legislature passed the Condon-Wadlin Act. Under this act, strikers could be considered as acting individually, and a public employee could lose his job for striking. Nevertheless, the Condon-Wadlin Act and the subsequent Taylor Law have failed to prevent strikes, mostly because the laws have not been enforced. Strikes, threats of strikes, and work slowdowns have become the main weapon of the new unionism. Nevertheless, the data show a trend away from the formal strike.

In departments covered by the Office of Collective Bargaining (OCB) there were twenty-one work stoppages between 1968 and 1979 lasting an average of four and a half days. In 1968 there were four work stoppages. The sanitation men's strike lasted eight days and involved 10,079 workers. The uniformed sanitation workers' union was fined $80,000 and its president, John DeLury, was fined $250.00 and sentenced to fifteen days in jail. The firemen and the oilers' local of the same union also struck the Sanitation Department. This strike lasted fourteen days, and the union was fined $8,000. In the same year lifeguards staged a one-day wildcat strike, and policemen had a rulebook slowdown; i.e., officers decided to work strictly according to rules, thus interrupting the normal flow of work. Under the Taylor Law, unions cannot be fined for wildcat strikes or job actions.

In 1970 and 1971 there was an increase in wildcat strikes. The elevator operators of Local No. 1 held a three-day wildcat strike. Correction officers in the Women's House of Detention had a one-day job action. In 1971 the city's uniformed police held a wildcat strike that involved 21,266 workers and lasted for six days. Social workers in the Human Resources Department also held a one-day wildcat strike. The two-day strike of the 7,000 bridge-tenders and sewage-plant workers affected many city departments.

In 1973, 450 welfare and clerical workers staged a two-day wildcat strike. Fourteen welfare guards held two wildcat strikes, of one and seven days respectively. In the same year, the 415 firemen conducted a five and one-half day strike for which they were fined $400,000. Each individual fireman participating in the strike was given one year of probation. In 1975, 6,900 members of the uniformed sanitation men's association struck for three days. Although no penalties were imposed on the union, individual strikers were fined and placed on one year of probation. Nurses at the Health and Hospitals Corporation and the uniformed officers at the Kings County Supreme Court both held one-day wildcat strikes.

There was a decline in the incidence of strikes between 1976 and 1979. Only one wildcat strike took place in 1976. It involved 18,000 nonprofessional workers in the Health and Hospitals Corporation and lasted four days. In 1978, 83 workers at the Human Resource Administration staged a three-day wildcat strike. In 1979, 1,300 corrections officers had a one-day wildcat strike. Finally, in that year 1,000 workers in the Off-Track Betting Corporation conducted a twenty-day wildcat strike.[13]

The data suggest that wildcat strikes are used in lieu of the formal strike because such actions involve fewer penalties and are easier to conduct. Although the antistrike laws have served to reduce formal strikes, they have not acted as a deterrent to work stoppages.

The Institutionalization of Collective Bargaining. Because of the mobilization effort by Wurf and his organizers, unions were in general able to play a key role in the mayoralty campaign of 1954. Mike Quill of the Transport Workers Union (TWU) worked hard for the election of Robert Wagner. In return, candidate Wagner promised to institute the collective-bargaining process for civil servants. When he assumed office, he had legislation passed to create a Department of Labor. This agency was not, however, exactly what the labor leaders had in mind, so they continued to deal with the state legislature instead. In July 1954, Wagner issued an interim order allowing workers the right to organize and be represented by their organizations and associations. The order also called for departments to establish joint union-management labor-relations committees.

These changes were major steps in organizing labor's relationship with the city, but union organizers and leaders sought still more concessions. In 1955, Wagner asked the Board of Estimate to allow workers a provision for a voluntary checkoff of union dues. (One must remember that at this time the unions had to collect dues by hand.) The so-called green authorization card stabilized the financial structure of the unions and made the unions heirs apparent to Tammany's political influence in the city.

In 1958, the entire process of collective bargaining was institutionalized by Executive Order 49. Now elections could be held to establish an exclusive bargaining agent for a group of employees. If an organization became the exclusive bargaining agent, its officials, shop stewards, and delegates could organize, meet, and counsel employees during working hours, and officers could conduct union business at the city's expense. Some departments even provided office space for the union delegates. Also, the entire grievance process became formalized. Collective bargaining and the checkoff authorization converted relatively weak labor organizations into powerful interest groups in city politics. As a result, the unions became more involved than ever in city politics, and vice versa.

The role of Mayor Wagner in the development of collective bargaining is critical to the understanding of union politics in New York. The ambitious Wagner came to office with strong family ties to the labor movement, dating back to Samuel Gompers. Wagner, like his father, supported progressive labor legislation. He also apparently thought that the way to strengthen the office of mayor was to institutionalize labor relations, so that the mayor, rather than the civil service commissioners, would become the focus of personnel administration and recruitment. The civil service he inherited was seventy years old, and its members, the middle class, could then boast of holding the balance of power in the electoral arena.

Because it was impossible to return to the partisan bureaucracy of the past, Wagner hoped to create a strong political organization from a loose group of civil servants. The concept of institutionalized unions as party surrogates was a major step in this direction. Jerry Wurf, not Tammany, had the troops. Tammany's patronage system was no longer appropriate after the advent of the welfare bureaucracy. So Wagner moved against the symbol of the genteel reformers, the Civil Service Commission, and rendered it politically impotent by appointing a professional director. The city personnel director would be the key to classification and other personnel matters.

The advent of the professional personnel director was seen as a triumph of the academic reformers, who were still calling for the end of the Civil Service Commission. Wagner then moved to coopt the unions by institutionalizing the checkoff system and establishing the Department of Labor. The purpose of the establishment of the Labor Department was to allow the mayor maximum flexibility in handling labor disputes. The union now had a stable financial base in exchange for political support. Wagner was then able to run again for reelection without the support of the regular party. He knew long before the election that the "party was over."

Wagner began to recruit high-ranking bureaucrats as running mates in his 1961 campaign, by which time the unionized city workers had finally replaced Tammany as the electoral force in the city. Wagner gained a reputation as a great labor mediator. This union-mayoral alliance helped him create an image as a man of vision. He apparently saw, before others did, the pressure on the union leaders for high wage settlements. Wagner declined to run in 1965. In retrospect, his labor policy has to be seen as the initiatory period in labor relations. It was not until after his retirement that the politicians began to lose control of the system. Professor Raymond Horton gives Wagner a mixed review:

Mayor Wagner's role in city labor relations was a complicated one. His forceful and effective opposition to union demands in collective bargaining obviously did not stem from any philosophical conception that public officials should not be dealing face-to-face with organized civil servants. It was after all, Wagner who had ushered New York City government into what was at that time a truly progressive stance with respect to city employees. Collective bargaining in the public sector was virtually unheard of in 1958. Wagner's interest in city employees was genuine, and his reforms between 1954 and 1958 were (as has been seen), at least in part based on the premise that the government long had treated its employees poorly.

At the same time, however, Wagner was not much interested in creating a labor relations system that would operate independently of his influence. Wagner's primary goal throughout his term was to enhance *his* control over the personnel system. Wagner understood the political implications of the labor relations program he set in motion not only for himself personally, but also for the office of the mayor. He also understood the degree of involvement in labor relations necessary for the maintenance of his influence in the system. He judged early that his own interest would be served by active participation in the program and acted accordingly throughout most of his final two terms in office.[14]

The dike was beginning to break.

With the welfare workers' strike of 1965, Wagner found himself unable to settle the dispute. By not appointing a tripartite panel of city officials, union leaders, and neutral experts, he was able to keep his reputation intact by accepting the settlement of the arbitrators. It seems as if Wagner viewed arbitration as a politically expedient device to be used after all other negotiations failed. Lindsay, his Republican successor, may have seen arbitration as an alternative to strikes and an opportunity to insulate the mayor's office from the give-and-take of labor mediation. Lindsay's solution to the labor problem was to institutionalize the collective-bargaining process even further.

The press hailed this move as a great reform, and some reformers saw it as taking politics out of labor relations. Lindsay's attempt at depoliticizing labor was not, however, well received by the labor community. Wagner had allowed labor leaders to posture and make points with the membership. Lindsay was trying to freeze them into a sterile professionalized agency called the Office of Collective Bargaining (OCB).

In 1969, Mayor Lindsay issued Executive Order No. 49, which created the tripartite Office of Collective Bargaining. The board included two labor members, two representatives from the city, and two members from the public. The board members determined the scope of bargaining, certified bargaining units, and supervised union elections.

Two years later, Lindsay recommended that the Collective Bargaining Office be given final authority to impose settlements on labor disputes.[15] This action institutionalized binding arbitration, and Lindsay apparently hoped that it would insulate him from the thicket of labor politics. It did not.

Professor Horton's evaluation of Mayor Lindsay's actions is revealing; he believes that Lindsay's delegation of responsibility for the labor-negotiation function to an agency was in part responsible for the turbulent labor relations during his administration.[16] Horton maintains that good labor relations are only possible with a strong management and an involved mayor. He feels that a third party tends to interrupt the free exchange of views and places the city at the mercy of unaccountable decision makers. There are, however, occasions where the public interest is served by the introduction of a facilitating third party. This is the case where the positions of the parties engaged in collective bargaining have become rigid, and neither can afford to appear to be losing. A labor leader may have promised more than he can deliver or a mayor stated publicly that he intends to hold a hard line on wage increases and productivity. In either case a face-saving device is indicated. Otherwise the city would be at the mercy of individuals acting out a drama for their respective constituencies.

Mediation and Arbitration. In an advanced unionized city such as New York, mediation, fact-finding, and arbitration have become institutionalized; i.e., procedures are spelled out in the legal code. Mediation involves a neutral third party, accepted by both sides, whose role is to facilitate the collective-bargaining process. Mediators cannot make decisions on their own, nor can they impose settlements. Their primary responsibility is to keep the negotiation talks on schedule and help set the agenda. They do this by focusing the attention of the parties on the issues at hand—previous commitments, costs of a particular proposal, the public interest—and on the relevant facts. If the talks break down, the mediators can call a meeting of the parties separately or in a group to discuss disputes.

Facilitating a compromise is not without its hazards. If the mediator is not careful, he may become the "lightning rod" for the frustrated participants, as was the case with Professor Walter Gelhorn, for example, in the 1980 transit strike. Presumably because mediators have no discernible economic or political interest in the outcome, they can approach issues less emotionally. Under the law the director of the Office of Collective Bargaining (OCB) can appoint mediation panels to facilitate the collective-bargaining process.

If mediation fails the parties can ask for an OCB impasse panel. Although the parties can determine the size and composition of the panel, only the OCB director can appoint the panel or the panel members. This fact-finding group will then study the facts in the dispute and recommend terms for a settlement. The recommendations may or may not be accepted. If they are rejected, the parties can appeal to the director of the OCB, and he can conduct yet another hearing and rule on the appropriateness of the panel's recommendations.

The goal of arbitration, however, is very different from mediation and fact-finding. It seeks to reach a settlement, not just a compromise. When parties have exhausted all attempts to settle, they may resort to binding arbitration, in which each party agrees to accept the ruling of the mediator.

There are basically two types of disputes submitted to arbitration: interest and rights. Interest disputes involve policy; that is, What shall be the basic terms and conditions of work? Rights disputes involve the interpretation or application of laws, agreements, or customary practices. Policy is usually made during collective bargaining and is rarely left to outside arbitration, whereas the arbitration of rights is built into the system. In New York, grievance and discipline procedures include as a last step binding arbitration. Labor contracts do not give arbitrators any power to modify a contract; rather, they apply interpretations to the provisions of the contract.

Despite its limitations many politicians see arbitration as a more rational alternative to collective bargaining. Professor David Lewin disagrees:

The arbitrator or impasse panel empowered to decide a settlement is concerned principally with the relationship between the two parties to the dispute and is not directly accountable to the public. Thus the arbitrator searches for a mutually acceptable "solution" that preserves the continuity of services. The cost of settlement is a subordinate objective, particularly in the absence of incentives for labor and management to agree among themselves. So-called "final-offer arbitration" tends to provide those incentives, but relatively few American governments use it.[17]

The stakes are high, and the participants are playing with the taxpayers' money and with bond-produced revenue.

Union Leaders, Politicians, and Elections. In New York the unions seized the fallen banner of Tammany during the second Wagner administration and began to act like the old kingmakers. The so-called civil service vote was to be delivered to Democratic candidates. The union bureaucracy claimed it could field an army of political canvassers to raise campaign funds and organize political campaigns. The leadership boasted that it could deliver votes from the membership and pull in those of members' relatives. No one studied whether or not union election activity ever persuaded civil servants to vote a particular way, or whether it influenced the votes of retired workers' families and friends. In addition no one seemed to know whether civil servants as a group voted more or less often than other groups.

The key for the union is not electioneering but endorsement. DeLury's endorsement of Vincent Impelletteri for mayor was supposed to have been the deciding factor in mobilizing this candidate of the Experience Party ticket to office. An endorsement from the PBA identifies a candidate as a conservative on law-and-order issues. The PBA endorsed James Buckley, the Conservative-Republican candidate, for the United States Senate in 1970. This endorsement may have helped Buckley to win a three-way race for the Senate seat. The endorsement gave the union a chance to show it was bipartisan. This is further evidence that Gomperism (i.e., the bipartisan approach advocated by the great labor leader Samuel Gompers) is beginning to emerge in city politics. Actually, the PBA is more interested in a candidate who advocates more police rather than a radical program to reduce crime. More police mean more dues and more members.

The restriction of civil servants' political activities by state and local laws served to formalize the payment of membership dues as a way of making political contributions. The neutral civil servant is a myth, as is the merit system.

Lobbying has become a skill among the employee organizations. They lobby for all causes, and at all levels of government. Few unionists in the private sector can boast of a better group of lobbyists, as Frank Havelick, a Koch administration aide, discovered in 1978–1979 when trying to get the state legislature to enact the mayor's civil service reform package. He claimed that "the unions have the best lobbyists in Albany." They also have been able to gather significant support from upstate Democrats and Republicans.

Public-sector unions have learned from the shortsightedness of their counterparts in the private sector. They leave no politician "unturned." Whether unions possess as much political power as has been claimed is open to question. Unions have been able to coopt many Democratic candidates and a few Republicans simply because the local party organizations were weak. This trend toward Gomperism may represent a good long-range strategy for union leaders. It does not make sense to paint all Republicans as antilabor or to allow one's organization to become the handmaiden of Democratic politicians.

Edward N. Costikyan, writer-politician, believes that labor-union leaders may be the new political bosses.[18] The truth is difficult to discern; a definitive voting-behavior analysis has not yet been made. But union leaders' claims for controlling primaries may have substance because few New Yorkers bother to vote at such times. Winning the Democratic nomination in the city is becoming tantamount to winning the general election. Republicans have not done well with unions, mainly because of the political posture they have to assume regarding budget matters. Any cut in personnel would mean loss of power for the union leadership. Political rhetoric about high government spending never sits well with union leaders because they must support candidates who promise an expansion of services.

Most political analysts who study unions have focused on the bargaining process itself. Actually the process of negotiation is in part an exercise in histrionics, in the symbols and rituals necessary to sell the public on the contract provisions. This is not to gainsay the substantive content of negotiations, but a considerable amount of time, money, and energy is invested in the drama itself.

Labor Negotiation as Drama. At first glance the scene of labor negotiation in the public sector resembles that of private industry. On one side of the bargaining table are the unions, represented by negotiating teams led by union presidents or executive directors and flanked by supporting staff. Labor leaders sometimes dress in sport shirts without ties and try to convince the audience that they are just working folks.

The press conference is critical to image building among labor leaders. At it the leaders try to make a case for the alleged economic hardship of their members, and warn in subtle and sometimes not so subtle ways of the consequences of the city's not agreeing to their terms. A closer examination reveals that the press conference sets the stage for the coming negotiations. Labor leaders have to be excellent actors as well as politicians. "Management"—i.e., the city's negotiation team—consists of mayoral appointees and aides—e.g., from the Office of Management and Labor Relations—and tries primarily to appear responsible, frugal, and humane. The representatives are often young lawyers who consider themselves specialists in labor relations. The initial press conferences are designed to reassure the public that the city is not going to give in to the union's demands. All that allegedly is wanted is a just and reasonable agreement that the city can afford. A closer look reveals these negotiators as stand-ins for the mayor and his budget director. Their mandate is to avoid political blunders, take care of nonwage agreements, and work out the language of the settlement.

The session begins with the union leaders presenting documented evidence that the city has the resources to grant wage increases consistent with inflation. In the initial meeting the union may present a list of member preferences. Some of the proposals have a Christmas-tree quality; i.e., all the items that the members hope to win in their lifetime. These proposals are critical to the negotiating process because they can be negotiated or traded away without damaging the image of the labor leaders.

The management team also presents a list of problems with the existing working contract and fiscal data. Recently management has presented a list of "givebacks"; i.e., items won in previous negotiations that are no longer affordable or desirable. Management usually asserts that the city can no longer afford "sweetheart work rules" and that there is need to establish productivity standards consistent with wage increases.

These initial positions are held until there is a breakdown in negotiations. A breakdown performs several functions: (1) it provides an opportunity for each side to present its case to the public; (2) it serves to reassure union membership that the leadership is taking a tough line at the negotiation table; (3) it allows the city negotiator to evaluate the "real" objectives of the union; and (4) it prepares the public to accept a compromise settlement.

A breakdown in negotiations without any interruption of services is, however, seldom sufficient to generate enough pressure for a settlement. A strike threat or work stoppage is then used as a facilitator. Under the pressure of a strike or a partial work stoppage, negotiations take on a new urgency, and participants are then able to include in the contract terms heretofore thought to be impossible. The end result is a "give-and-take" compromise agreement that allows management and union leaders to argue that each side got the best possible deal.

As in any live performance there are mistakes and miscalculations for "going public" is not without its pitfalls. The audience may become angry and bored. Some negotiations similarly have a way of staying too long before the public. Unions, however, seem aware of their audience's time and patience.

The truth-in-bargaining theme is critical to the negotiating enterprise. Each side must negotiate in good faith. The city should not make agreements using a Trojan horse, nor should the union seek contract commitments which the city may not be able to afford. On the other hand, the public is not served by promises of productivity and efficiency which neither the city nor the union can implement.

Elected city officials must condemn strikes even when they know that they are necessary to sell contract packages to the public. Often contracts are so costly that management must appear to have been forced into them.

The hidden agenda of any negotiating session is the reelection of union leaders and city officials and the concern each party has for its place in history. Both parties must try to save face and reach an agreement because to do otherwise would expose too much of their personalities and policies to the public. Such exposure would also invite more criticism as well as interference from the courts, along with state officeholder participation in the negotiations.

Finally, the end of a successful negotiation is seen as a triumph for the negotiators. The media praise their statesmenship. The public is then allowed to breathe a sigh of relief. Services resume, and the parties begin preparations for the next round in the contract cycle.

The Role of Unions in Vertical Recruitment. Mancur Olson, an economist, has argued that industrial and often private-sector unions are by-products of the expansion of the economy. He claims that these organizations grew only after they abandoned their political ambitions and concentrated on collective bargaining. The imposition of compulsory membership—closed shop—and the service incentives, i.e., insurance and seniority privileges, offered by the unions enabled them to recruit new members and become a more effective lobby within the political system.

Olson's explanation for the growth of unions applies to some extent to the history of New York City's public-employee organizations. Under the so-called old unionism, public-employee organizations remained small and generally ineffective. With the advent of the new unionism, checkoff authorization, and collective bargaining, the organizations grew and prospered. It could thus be argued that District Council 37 is a product of the expansion of city services and jobs. Nonetheless, this is where the analogy ends. Public-service unions are subject to market forces, but they are not restricted by them. In the private sector, union leaders' demands are regulated by the competitive marketplace.

In their negotiation with management, unions must take care not to deprive the company of a competitive edge. Unreasonable wage demands can undermine profit margins and force a company out of business. Government, on the other hand, is a monopoly and not a part of any competitive marketplace. The chances of a city government's going out of business are remote. Without the restraint of the market, union leaders can demand and obtain higher wage settlements.

A work stoppage by public employees is usually more disruptive than strikes in the private sector. The 1980 New York City transit strike succeeded in disrupting traffic for nearly all city residents. It demonstrated that fiscal uncertainties are not an effective deterrent to costly work stoppages. The Metropolitan Transit Authority (MTA) negotiators were not able to convince union leaders to accept lower increases in wages or to make work-rule concessions. Many work rules, negotiated during relatively good times, have become millstones around the city's neck.

Labor leaders have labeled concessions on work rules as givebacks. The media focused much attention on winning givebacks as a signal of a tougher management stance toward unions.

During the negotiations it became apparent that this strategy was failing, and that the union was going to receive substantial increases in pay and retain concessions won in previous negotiations. The first week proved that the union could hold out longer than management. The public, distracted at first by the novelty of community cooperation, demanded near the end of the week that the subway should run regardless of cost. The public seemed prepared to accept a ten-cent increase in fare without a corresponding improvement in service.

The collapse of the MTA negotiation team compromised any chance that the mayor may have had to present a new tough image to the remaining city unions. The subsequent city-wide negotiations saw the other employees receive substantial increases without resorting to a work stoppage.

In retrospect the "giveback strategy" proved to be an unfortunate one. It was the wrong strategy for three reasons: First, the notion of givebacks leads the public to believe that city negotiators are the equal of their labor counterparts. They are not, and cannot effectively demand anything beyond symbolic gestures from unions. Secondly, the giveback tactic perpetuates the idea that nonwage items involve no cost. In fact, employees who get days off, passes for subways, extra holidays, and the like, add to the cost of delivering services.

The giveback strategy is also weak because it runs counter to labor-union tradition. Union leaders cannot make concessions to management because they might appear as appeasement to the membership. Many workers now feel that the privileges won in previous years are non-negotiable. This assumption is made because in interviews workers did not see the connection between a possible taxpayer revolt and the content of their contracts. Private-sector unions have only made such concessions when the life of the company was in jeopardy. Public-sector unions do not have to worry about the perils of the marketplace. For this reason they do not seem to possess any inhibitory mechanism. Konraḍ Lorenz in *On Aggression* has argued that such a mechanism prevents homicide among animals of the same species.[19] Human beings are the only animals known to engage in wholesale destruction or homicide. It is ironic that public unions born in the public domain would be so unconcerned about public reactions or service deterioration.

The giveback strategy makes sound economic sense. If some way could be found to eliminate these rules and privileges, real savings could accrue from less overtime, administrative delay, and work-schedule manipulations. Nonetheless the ability of unions to maintain sweetheart work rules in a fiscal crisis supports the view that unions are successful because they have increased the autonomy of bureaucrats, and have given them a city-subsidized political organization. City workers now have a politicized, external interest group working full-time for their interests. This perfect marriage of interest combines the role of unions as party surrogates with that of the managers of the large fringe-benefit funds generated by civil servants. In addition the unions perform the following equally important functions:

1. Lobbying in Washington, Albany, and City Hall for the goals of service and job expansion.

2. Mobilizing public demands and support for program-expansion policy (i.e., shaping attentive public opinion).

3. Managing internal-organization incentives (i.e., insurance, work schedule, seniority privileges) and sanctions (i.e., assisting in disciplining workers).

4. Providing communication with workers at other levels of government.

5. Socializing new workers and new local politicians.

6. Simplifying public issues regarding the bureaucracy.

In order to perform these functions, unions have developed large and professional staffs. These staffs have become critical of the political goals of the city bureaucracy. Many union staff members serve as members of city-agency advisory groups, and are consulted when commissioners are chosen or dismissed. They work in the campaigns of local politicians and serve as their advisers. In summary, the impact of unions upon public policy is direct and substantial. Their role is the result of the critical brokerage functions they perform while promoting the interests of the city bureaucracy. In the 1950s, Wallace Sayre and Herbert Kaufman observed a more limited function:

The impact of the organized bureaucracies and their leaders upon public policy is largely indirect. It is achieved often through the separate actions of the individual bureaucrats as members of the departments and agencies of the city government. But the nexus between the leaders of the organized bureaucracies and the actions of the bureaucrats in the formal governmental hierarchy is a strong and important one: it is the leaders who have largely created the climate of autonomy and the values of the closed bureaucracies within which the individual bureaucrats express their preferences and exercise their influence in public policy.[20]

SUMMARY

The unionization of New York City civil servants is perhaps the most important political and economic development in the evolution of the city bureaucracy. The trade-union leaders have become the new political kingmakers in the city.

Group theorists or pluralists have attempted to define these new-comers to the urban arena as a natural part in the process of group-interest articulation and aggregation. Sociologist Arthur Bentley and political scientist David Truman promoted the view that individuals join organizations because of shared interests.[21] Economist Mancur Olson believes that individuals join to receive separate and selective incentives. These benefits are only available to official members of a group. New York unions have partially met this requirement by providing exclusive representation, continuing education, job-referral advocacy, political research, candidate selection and campaigning. They also provide legal aid and opportunities for social recognition.

Professor Olson believes that private-sector unions are a by-product of industrial activities. From a review of the evolution of unions in New York, it appears that public-sector unions are a by-product of the growth and expansion of the service economy. Mutual benefit associations were transformed into unions in their attempt to obtain better wages and work rules from the political parties. Adaptation of the private-sector trade-unionist model to city government is still in the process of adjustment. The public is still upset by the striking of firemen or the police. Nonetheless it is fair to say that unions will continue to develop as the city recruits better-educated workers in search of higher pay and social recognition.

The New York unions were able to fill the political vacuum left by the decline of political parties and the middle-class reform-oriented politics of the city. Olson is correct when he asserts that unions gained stability only after abandoning their political orientation and concentrating on collective bargaining, ergo, abandoning old unionism for new. He adds that "it was only when the labor unions started to deal with employers who alone had the power to *force* the workers to join the union that they began to prosper."[22]

Sayre, Kaufman, and their student Raymond Horton have accepted the group theorists' notion of group conflict among competing interest groups as the defining process of decision making in New York. Implicit in this notion is the view that political equilibrium rises out of this particular pattern of interaction. The influence of employee unions is somewhat counterbalanced by the existence of other groups. Sayre and Kaufman's study meticulously describes most of the interest groups in the New York political arena.

Pluralists believe that public policy is made incrementally through the resolution of group conflict by bargaining, negotiation, and compromise. Pluralists also believe that it is important for these conflicts to be resolved within the arena itself, and not through the intervention of some outside force. Horton's study of unions illustrates how issues resolved through arbitration by an outside force can have serious implications for the collective-bargaining process and for the political process as well.

The advent of unions as a surrogate political-party system has tended to increase fragmentation in the making of public policy. Because union leaders need to win good contracts to stay in power, the city has been forced to borrow large sums of money and raise taxes and fees to meet the escalating wage demands of the union membership. In order to pay its employees, the city must continue a dubious policy of borrowing from Peter to pay Paul.

Overlapping membership in departments and unions has affected organizational behavior in the bureaucracy. The unions make few demands on their members, and members see little conflict between their jobs and union membership. It may be argued that unions have been used by city workers to gain higher income and more job security, and to protect themselves from public criticism. Union leaders have also learned to coexist with the informal organizations within city departments. Conflicts between unions and the more informal groups are rare.

The city government has not served as a countervailing force to the union leadership. Politicians as a group are restrained by the electoral threat that unions pose. Antiunion politics has consistently proved to be bad politics. Many union members never forgave Mayor Lindsay, for instance, for his initial tough posture with respect to union politics. Lindsay never recovered from the transit strike, despite his subsequent concessions to union leadership. Through the institutionalization of the bargaining process, he did succeed, however, in linking the fate of union leaders to that of politicians.

Union leaders have been asked to become members of various governmental boards and committees. This change means that union leaders help in the shaping of city policies which their members implement. As a consequence, they now find it difficult to criticize their sponsored politicians. The position taken by Mayor Koch, with regard to hospital closings and civil service reform, puts him in a combative posture toward unions. His "I am not going to be pushed around by unions" strategy was very effective during the 1980 transit strike. If he continues this posture for other contract negotiations, the unions will almost surely be forced to make adjustments in their script to fit his personality and serve their own interests.

5

THE NEW FISCAL MANAGERS
AND THE PERSONNEL ARENA

Writing about New York's 1975 fiscal crisis requires an open mind because the events were in perpetual flux. A scorecard might be useful in keeping straight the continuous changes among the political actors and interest groups. The city changed mayors and fiscal advisers after the advent of the crisis. The old-line politicians and bureaucrats were replaced and displaced by the various boards and committees studying the city's financial status. More power now lies with political appointees, who are not accountable to the public.

The new men in charge of the crisis determined who got what and how much in the city. Fiscal choices were no longer made by men on loan from corporations or universities. The result is urban government by budgeteers rather than by top economic leaders, such as those described in Floyd Hunter's *Community Power Structure.* "Political budgeteers" were the new actors on the personnel scene. They threatened both the brokers—i.e., unions—and the politicians.

Nature of the Fiscal Crisis: Insider View. Not only was there no agreement about the actual dollar amounts involved in the debt of New York City, but there were and are arguments about the very nature of the fiscal crisis itself. Many blamed the banks for failing to bail the city out of its obvious fiscal perils. But most adhered to what may be called the conventional-wisdom thesis, which states that the fiscal crisis was caused by a weak tax base, incompetent politicians, and a too generous welfare system.

Politicians did not stand up to the demands of the employees' unions, this argument runs. The state legislature did not resist the demands of the city for more borrowing power. There was no control over the fiscal management of the city—the state's biggest revenue source. The state comptroller did not sound the budgetary alarm with sufficient vigor. The press did not question any of the fiscal policies before the crisis. Public-employee unions, having assumed a surrogate political-party role, committed themselves to city policies that were at variance with the public interest. The political-party system was too fragmented to be an effective vehicle for mobilization of support in the state legislature or in Congress. The argument also asserts that the New York City congressional delegation, one of the most divided and ineffective in Congress, was unable to build the necessary coalition to secure passage of a program for long-term aid to the city.

A converging trend was the general economic decline of the city. The decline of the economy meant a corresponding decline in the city's tax base. Without an adequate tax base the city's revenues could not keep pace with expenditures. Therefore a major fiscal crisis was inevitable.

The Fiscal Observer, a New York City magazine, blamed a variety of ills for the city fiscal crisis. It asserted:

First, the city's expenses paid for out of tax levy mushroomed, increasing at a 9.9% average annual rate in 1960–65, 11.4% in 1965–70 and 15.0% in 1970–75. From 1960 to 1970, full-time city employment grew by 43% and municipal union membership by 300%. In 1960, a mere 324,200 people received public assistance (4% of the city's population). In 1970, this was up to 1,094,700 people (14%).

Second, city revenues did not keep up with this expenditure burden, partly because of the downturn in the city economy in the 1970s and partly because of a reluctance to raise city tax rates. The city's unemployment rate jumped 4.8% in 1970 to 10.6% in 1975. Wage and salary employment in the city dropped 13%, from 3,797,700 in 1969 to 3,287,800 in 1975, while municipal employment rose by 30,000. Third, the city covered up its budget deficits by putting operating expenses in its capital budget (nearly $1 billion in 1975), overestimating its anticipated intergovernmental aid and real estate tax revenues, issuing and rolling over into subsequent fiscal years an excessive amount of short-term debt, skimming money from its pension funds, and other fiscal abuses.[1]

Stated another way, if federal and state aid were not included, the expenditures from 1973 through 1975 exceeded the revenues of the city by a ratio of two to one. The city reported an $8,157 billion cumulative deficit on June 30, 1975. Although the debt was reduced to $2.5 billion two years later, this was a massive sum for a city with a declining tax base.[2]

Another problem was the growing cost of personnel maintenance. The largest item in the city budget, estimated at 75 percent, included growing costs for retired city workers. The city had an unfunded accrued-pension liability that exceeded $7 billion in fiscal year 1976—in addition to the $2.5 billion deficit in mid-1977. In other words, the city had mortgaged its financial future to pay pension and benefit obligations to its employees. In order to carry out a successful rescue operation, the city had therefore either to generate more revenues or reduce its commitments.

Perhaps the most telling economic statistic was the increasing number of businesses leaving the city. As Herbert Bienstock, the former regional director for the U.S. Department of Labor, who collected data on the economic health of the city, observed:

The job loss of recent years brought employment in New York City in 1975 to the lowest level in the 25 years data have been available for the city. The experience of the last six years reflects the substantial weakness in virtually all major sectors of the city's economy. Factory employment, which dropped by an average of 11,000 jobs a year for a total loss of 213,000 between 1950 and 1969, was off at an average of 43,000 annually or 257,000 between 1969 and 1975. In 1975, factory employment in New York City was down over ½ million from its peak level of 1947 to a current level of slightly over ½ million. The private nonmanufacturing sector, which added 370,000 jobs or an average of 19,000 a year between 1950 and 1969, subsequently lost over 200,000 jobs or 34,000 annually in the last six years.[3]

Factory employment, a key element in utilizing the unskilled manpower of a city, had become almost nonexistent in New York. Businesses that employed large numbers of semiskilled workers were now located in the Sun Belt—the urban centers of the South and Southwest—or in the suburbs. The new immigrants to New York City, unlike their predecessors, could not use either the factories or the docks to achieve social and economic upward mobility. The result was an enormous waste of human resources and a permanent class of unemployables. Although the city still led the nation in the financial investment and communications industries, its future prospects as an employer of great masses of workers were dim.[4]

Another area of lost jobs was in corporate industry. From 1969 to 1975 the city lost 100,000 jobs because of the removal of wholesale and retail industries to the suburbs. New York City was not only losing jobs, but also corporate office headquarters. In a 1971 study, the Chase Manhattan Bank's Economic Research Division identified American Can (2,000 employees), Foster Wheeler (1,500) and Shell Oil (2,500) as examples from the list of *Fortune* 500 companies that had left the city. They went to Greenwich, Connecticut; Livingston, New Jersey; and

Houston, Texas, respectively. Although a majority of the twenty-two companies moved within the tri-state area, they represented a loss of New York City jobs.[5]

In 1978 a study by Columbia University's Conservation of Human Resources Project found that corporate headquarters provided one-fifth of the city's employment (586,000 jobs) and one-fourth of the city's pay ($8.7 billion). Only 62 of the 128 company headquarters listed in the *Fortune* 500 list in 1965 were still in the city in 1975. During this time, 28 new *Fortune* 500 companies came to the city while 7 former "500" companies remained in the city.[6]

Losing these *Fortune* 500 headquarters was an ominous sign of the city's decline as a competitor for the nation's office-building real estate. This decline continued despite the fact that the city possessed the nation's most-developed cultural amenities. Newer cities, especially those in the South and Southwest, were able to lure business headquarters away because of their low energy, labor, and building costs. New York City's position as an attractive location for corporations was further eroded by the establishment of international airports in the Sun Belt region.

If the days of the city as a center of manufacturing, trade, and office headquarters seemed numbered, its reputation as the most advanced human-services system in the nation was also showing signs of wear. The city's enormous welfare-industry complex was aging. This complex, stimulated by the public-sector expansion of "The War on Poverty" and the demand for equal opportunities for members of its minority communities, was manned by some of the highest-paid civil servants in the nation. The *Fiscal Observer* reported that from 1960 to 1970, full-time city employment grew by 45 percent and municipal union membership by 300 percent.

Recruiting and paying civil servants proved to be an easier task than integrating them. Even with the expanding economy, minorities found city department doors closed to them.

Table 5.1 shows that minority—black and Puerto Rican—representation in the work force was small and concentrated in the newer city agencies. Through their unions and seniority systems, white workers were able to restrict most minority members to recently established agencies, such as the Health and Hospitals Corporation, the Human Resources Administraiton, and the Board of Education. The lack of any percentage increase in minority employment in hospitals and sanitariums supports this view. Human-services departments, which operated some programs with federal grant-in-aid monies, attempted to integrate minorities with varying degrees of success. Of these agencies, the Board of Education was the most successful; it had a 12 percent

TABLE 5.1: Representation of Blacks and Puerto Ricans by Function of City Government, 1963 and 1971

Function	1963					1971				
	Total No. Employees	Black No.	Black Percent	Puerto Rican No.	Puerto Rican Percent	Total No. Employees	Black No.	Black Percent	Puerto Rican No.	Puerto Rican Percent
Financial Administration and General Control	12,059	1,825	15	203	2	10,308	2,139	21	283	3
Streets and Highways	4,251	297	7	28	1	4,006	461	12	73	2
Public Welfare	10,485	4,218	40	394	4	23,237	10,304	44	1,350	6
Police Protection	NOT AVAILABLE					35,570	3,332	9	923	3
Fire Protection	13,320	554	4	38	*	14,873	614	4	91	1
Natural Resources, Parks and Recreation	5,693	774	14	77	1	4,895	939	19	103	2
Hospitals and Sanitariums	34,511	18,720	54	2,637	8	40,646	22,022	54	3,935	10
Health	4,560	1,675	37	109	2	6,558	2,293	35	443	7
Housing Services	11,133	3,417	31	954	9	15,703	5,250	33	2,500	16
Planning and Development	174	15	9	1	*	410	51	12	3	1
Corrections	2,910	1,036	36	46	2	3,681	1,600	43	131	4
Utilities and Transportation	4,393	264	6	35	1	5,650	382	7	88	2
Sanitation and Sewage	13,890	1,088	8	67	*	15,414	1,917	13	319	2
Education	55,840	6,108	11	708	1	88,641	16,303	18	5,101	6
Human Services	NOT AVAILABLE					1,940	1,047	54	254	13

Source: The Employment of Minorities, Women and the Handicapped in City Government: A Report of a 1971 Survey, New York City Commission on Human Rights, p. 18.
*Indicates less than one percent.

increase in minority employees. The old-line organizations, such as the fire, the police, and the sanitation departments resisted employing minorities. The percentage (4 percent) of minorities in fire protection remained the same over the years. There were, however, important increases among the sanitation and sewage workers.

Insiders believe that no ethnic group can escape the perils of a declining economy. Seniority can only protect workers if there is money to pay them. When the city loses its private economic base, the public economic base also deteriorates.

The picture that emerged was one of a city that could not retain manufacturing, service, and shipping industries, losing them to the suburbs and the Sun Belt cities. When industry and jobs move out, people eventually follow.

To reverse this trend, some insiders argued that the city must alter its tax structure, build industrial parks—by changing the zoning laws—and improve the safety of its streets. Unquestionably policy makers would find these changes extremely difficult to accomplish. An example of the difficulties involved may be termed the "Nabisco syndrome." Nabisco moved from New York City to Hanover, New Jersey, in 1975. Hanover was quiet and green, but it did not have the workers that Nabisco needed. Thus the company had to bus its skilled bakers in from the so-called ghettos.

Why could not Nabisco have located its plant in Harlem or Brooklyn? There were several vacant lots large enough to house it. The company did not move to Harlem—where many of its workers were—because of tax, crime, and zoning problems. The economic conditions in poor communities then and now are part of a vicious cycle. Companies do not locate in such communities because of crime, zoning laws, and taxes; the crime problem in such communities is at least partly the result of unemployment; the taxes are high because unemployment requires large people-serviced bureaucracies; landlords' and politicians' attempts to keep their power base have maintained strict residential zoning codes.

In short, the insiders' view was that the city had become a victim of its liberal welfare policy and the declining need for unskilled labor. Because the city's public-sector economy could not sustain itself, the city was forced to borrow to pay its debt. This arrangement barely survived the sixties and could not withstand the inflation of the seventies.

The Nature of the Fiscal Crisis: Outsiders' View. The Congressional Budget Office (CBO) divided the causes of the 1975 fiscal crisis into two classifications: short-term factors and long-range factors.[7] The short-term factors included the loss of investor confidence in the credit worthiness of the city. Since investing is not an exact science, investors rely on psychological and environmental factors in making investment decisions. Rumors of pending financial problems frightened off potential New York City investors.

The other short-range problem was the market cycle itself. CBO reported data that 1975 was an especially heavy municipal borrowing period. In such a period, New York City could not compete with other borrowers. Recession and an unprofitable bond market also reduced the number of investors. Many commercial banks withdrew from the bond market, thus reducing further the number of potential customers for city notes.

Two related factors were the lack of small investors and the nature of municipal bond markets. If municipal bonds were available in small denominations, perhaps many average New Yorkers might have invested in them out of love for the city. (Unfortunately municipal bonds are only available in large denominations. It takes large investment firms and commercial banks to accommodate their cash requirements.) The CBO report also pointed out another factor operating in the market. It observed that "the market for New York City securities is concentrated largely in New York State where the interest is exempt from not only federal but also state and local taxes. This market may be close to saturated by the large quantities of state and city securities outstanding. To broaden the market to nonstate residents would require interest rates sufficiently high to compensate for the fact that non-New York holders would have to pay state income taxes on the interest earned from their New York City securities."[8]

The recession and the decline in the tax base of the city proved to be serious impediments to the attractiveness of city bonds. The city was also hurt by its reliance on sales and income taxes as the primary source of revenue. CBO argued that the property tax was a more stable revenue source.

The impact of the recession on New York's sales-tax base is illustrated by the following statement:

Despite a 9.3 percent increase in consumer prices in the year ending June 30, 1975, the volume of taxable sales in the city rose by only 1.7 percent. In New York even the property tax has proven to be unreliable. Delinquencies have risen rapidly from 4.2 percent of collections in fiscal year 1970 to 7.2 percent currently.

The recession has caused high unemployment and stationary incomes which have increased the city's expenditure requirements as well as undercut its expected revenue growth. Not only have the numbers of families eligible for welfare programs increased, but it is also likely that the demand for other city services, such as hospitals, has been boosted by the recession because fewer city residents are able to afford the costs of the alternative private institutions.[9]

The long-term factors that caused the fiscal crisis include the inability of the city to provide employment for migrants in need of unskilled and semi-skilled jobs. The lack of jobs created a large welfare-recipient population. The situation was exacerbated by the white flight (i.e., middle-class white suburbanization) and a corresponding decline in the tax base. The CBO reported that $3.5 billion or approximately one-third of city spending was welfare-related. Whereas in other urban counties the cost of providing such services is shared by all government units, New York City because of its merger of county and city government absorbed all costs.

CBO concluded that the city was unique in that it had a larger recalcitrance debt which necessitated more borrowing. The city continually needed to go to the market for funds. The recalcitrance debt continued regardless of the health of the city's economy. Finally CBO concluded that the city economy was extremely sensitive to the business cycle.

The CBO's conclusions were cogent particularly since they blamed market forces for the ills of the city rather than individual or relatively powerful interest groups. Somehow the city officials emerge as altruistic, perhaps too kind to migrants and welfare recipients. They were presented as shortsighted bankers. There is nothing so persuasive as conventional wisdom writ statistically.

An alternative thesis to the outsiders' view was that problems of New York were not tax-related. This thesis argued that neither welfare recipients nor the bond market caused the financial problems of the city. It focused on the closing paragraph of the CBO report which stated that New York City's economy was particularly sensitive to changes in the business cycle (i.e., the financial investment cycle). If the insiders' and outsiders' views can be called conventional wisdom, then the alternative may be termed unconventional wisdom.

Unconventional wisdom asserted that policies which were reported as causes of the crisis were really symptoms of the problem. The real economic problem of the city was more structural. That is to say, the city was the first urban center to encounter major changes in the nation's economic foundations. America was no longer a competitive industrial power. Its decline as an industrial power was precipitated by (1) internationalization of small and large manufacturing enterprises (e.g., the garment industries in Southeast Asia); (2) development of foreign economic influences (e.g., OPEC); (3) the instability of the nation's currency—making other currency more reliable and attractive to investors; (4) worldwide inflationary factors caused by both market forces and political manipulations; and (5) rising income expectations for workers worldwide.

New York City was also challenged as an economic market by other major American metropolitan centers. Cities, such as Houston and Atlanta, had space, pliant zoning laws, amenable tax structures, and a nonunion workforce. All these factors converged to facilitate a new fiscal alignment in the city. The fiscal crisis was a necessary event to force the public to rethink policy and rewards toward extant interest groups.

What Is Fiscal Alignment? Fiscal alignment occurs when there is a major shift of economic resources from one set of interest groups to another. The shift in the urban economy produced a corollary shift in the determinants of public policy. Since urban personnel policies are based on short and long-term commitments of government expenditures, any realignment of these monies causes a corresponding change in the array of relevant interest groups. Such realignments usually occur in reaction to pronounced downturns in the national economy.

The relevant realignment periods for New York City in this century were the Great Depression of the 1930s and the recession of the 1950s. In the thirties the LaGuardia administration realigned the city's public-sector economy by agreeing to make changes throughout the civil service and to reduce patronage jobs. Mayor LaGuardia also negotiated a refinancing of the city's debt with the city investors. The so-called Banker Agreement of 1933 saved the city from default.

Robert Wagner faced an economic crisis of a different kind. Labor-organizing activities of the late fifties and early sixties caused another change in the civil service. To offset costly strikes, Wagner integrated the uniformed associations (i.e., fire and police) and other public-employee union leaderships into the administrative decision-making structure of the city. The "green-card authorization," allowing workers to check off their union dues, gave the unions a stable financial base and enabled them to build stronger organizations. In effect, Mayor Wagner created a surrogate political organization to replace Tammany Hall. However, these organizations required large wage increments to keep their members happy. Public-employee salaries and wages became a major part of the city budget.

After the 1965 strike, which Wagner could not settle by traditional means of negotiation, he abandoned collective bargaining for binding arbitration. Arbitration, unlike negotiation, precludes political accountability. Arbitrators, who are not elected by union members or the public, often see their role as firemen settling strikes at any cost. Wagner also had a law passed that gave him authority to issue more Revenue Anticipatory Notes (RANs) to cover the widening fiscal gap of the city. This proved to be a temporary solution, as soon became evident from the expensive settlement that resulted from the transit-union contract negotiations. Wagner decided not to run for reelection and to let the new mayor find the money to pay the wage settlements.

Mayor Lindsay's solution was to transfer and defer operating costs to the capital budget. This had the effect of putting a cap on the boiling fiscal pot. When ex-Budget Director and City Comptroller Abraham Beame was elected to the mayor's office in 1973, the pliant accounting system that he had helped to create while serving in office previously began to show an enormous cash-flow problem for the city treasury.

In March 1975, fifteen months after Beame took office as mayor, the city's fiscal star went supernova. The city investment counselors refused to certify city notes because of the lack of proper documentation of municipal revenues. On April 1, Standard and Poor's, the security-rating firm, withdrew its high rating for New York City bonds, and the investment community stopped handling the city's notes. The nation's largest municipality was struck by a full-blown fiscal crisis.

The Ford administration, with its eyes on the next presidential election (1976), decided to refuse to give New York the massive amount of aid that it would need to stave off bankruptcy, thus, it hoped, currying favor with the rest of the country. But Gerald Ford did not anticipate the resourcefulness of the communications center of the world. The New York media made the President look callous, sanctimonious, and insensitive to the city's plight. The press even reported the concern of Western European nations about the effects of the New York fiscal crisis on their economies. Finally, the President decided to lend the city the money to get it through its short-term cash-flow crisis, but he refused to sign the public-works bill that would have delayed the fiscal realignment or made it less painful. Part of the lending agreement was that New York State would closely supervise the financial transactions of the city. The state responded by creating watchdog agencies and relegating the elected city government to almost exile status.

Creatures of the Fiscal Crisis. There were a multitude of civic and political committees studying the city's fiscal crisis. The Municipal Assistance Corporation and the Emergency Financial Control Board, however, could do no more than make recommendations. The Municipal Assistance Corporation (MAC) was designed to sell $3 billion worth of long-term bonds (fifteen years) to pay off the city's short-term debt. Figure 5.2 identifies the holders and the distribution of the investors.[10]

FIGURE 5.2: Holders of City and MAC Debt,
Sept. 30, 1975, and Sept. 30, 1977 ($ in Millions)

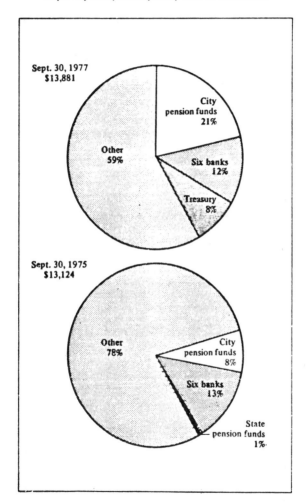

Sources: Office of City Comptroller; MAC; offices of
state funds' comptrollers; Senator Proxmire report,
March 29, 1978.

Figure 5.2 suggests that the variety of bond holders of city debt was shrinking. The pension funds (e.g., the New York City Employees' Retirement System, Teachers' Retirement System, Policy Pension Funds, and Fire Department Pension Fund) invested $2 billion in the city and MAC bonds debt. The city's banking community invested $1.6 billion, or 12 percent of the city debt. The general investment community invested $10 billion or 78 percent as of September 30, 1975, and thus held $8 billion of all the city and MAC debt.[11] Most of the subsequent financial plans of the city assumed a continued investment by these groups. A federal loan guarantee would make it easier for these groups to invest. A loan guarantee would also facilitate the reselling of city bonds and notes to other investors.

The New York City debt had become big business, and stretching the debt (i.e., arranging long-term payments) required skills possessed only by individuals trained in the intricacies of high finance and investment. For this reason and others, the MAC Board, known as "Big Mac," was dominated by businessmen and investment experts. The board had nine voting members or directors, five chosen by the governor, four by the mayor. There were six nonvoting representatives appointed by the New York State Legislature, the New York City Board of Estimate, and the majority leaders of the City Council. The corporation got its funds from the state sales tax and the stock-transfer tax collected in the city. The state comptroller was to audit the city's books and issue a report on the city's compliance with the corporation requirements. The city in turn was to report its fiscal health to Big Mac. Big Mac's ultimate weapon in obtaining city fiscal records and documentation was something called "determination of noncompliance." The city could not afford to ignore MAC requests for information because the government had a stake in creating a good fiscal image. Aside from marketing bonds, the essential purpose of Big Mac was to assure investors that they would make money, and to tell the public that the city had discontinued its former accounting procedures.

The city had to make some difficult personnel and service policy choices. The authority of MAC and new state-imposed limitations on short-term borrowing gave the city little room to negotiate with the various interest groups. City officials had the unenviable task of explaining cutbacks and service reductions to the public. Elected city officials were helped in this task by Felix Rohatyn, perhaps the best-known of the city's new fiscal managers.

Rohatyn, as chairman of MAC and a member of the Emergency Financial Control Board, emerged as the major spokesman for the new fiscal-restraint policy. An articulate investment banker, he dazzled news reporters and talk-show hosts with figures and soothsayings about the city's chances against bankruptcy. The outside world saw him not as a typical politician but as a businessman coming to rescue the city. Rohatyn lived up to his billing. He was a joy to listen to, and he had the image the city so desperately needed. With Rohatyn's performance, the fiscal manager's role gained a model and an important place in the city's political theater.

The Emergency Financial Control Board (EFCB) was created by the legislature in 1975 to monitor the fiscal affairs of the city. Its members included the governor, mayor, state and city controllers, and three members from private business. The governor was the chairman of EFCB and he was assisted by a special deputy state comptroller who supervised the fiscal decisions of the city. The mayor was mandated to present a four-year fiscal plan to the board. If he did not, the board could impose one on the city. The board questioned city expenditures and union contracts, recommended replacement of city officials, and generally attempted to manage city fiscal policy. In effect the city was in quasi-receivership. The board took all city revenue into its own bank accounts and disbursed funds in accordance with the four-year plan.

Steven Berger, a lawyer and former director of the Scott Commission under Governor Nelson Rockefeller, was appointed executive director of the EFCB by Hugh Carey in March 1976 and quickly became a controversial figure. The press described him as a "hatchet man" sent by Governor Carey to put the city's financial affairs in order. Berger seemed to relish the role and made a series of tough statements to the press, whereupon the media became fascinated by his personality and rhetoric. The local public television station (WNET) did a special feature on him. His name was mentioned as a possible mayoral candidate. With the Berger performance, the fiscal managers became involved in the day-to-day management of the city. This was short-lived, however, as Berger had to compromise more and more with the unions and other politically influential groups, culminating in his finally leaving the job and embarking upon his own consulting career.

In effect, the fiscal crisis created two new celebrities—Rohatyn and Berger—as role models for the new ascendent group. The next leadership of the fiscal managerial class could choose to follow the dispassionate style of Rohatyn or adopt the tough-guy image of Berger. The new fiscal managers also needed to develop a more political rhetoric to legitimate their claims to power and resources.

The new managers' principal political vehicles, MAC and EFCB, became firmly entrenched as fiscal oversight bureaucracies. These organizations may survive for several years, albeit with name changes and more participation on the boards from other interest groups. According to Newfield and DuBrul, the lack of representation on the boards of MAC and EFCB was a serious problem. They argued:

The most striking deficiency of the whole structure is that it is unrepresentative. The memberships were negotiated and screened by bankers whose primary concern was the market. . . . There is no labor-union representative on either board. . . . There is no Hispanic representative on either board. There is no participant who clearly identifies with the point of view of the small homeowner, who has mortgage payments to make and is worried about his job at the plant, and how he is ever going to finance three kids through college. There is no resident of Brooklyn or Queens, the city's most populous boroughs, where most of the city's lower middle class live out an alienated existence. There is no neighborhood activist on either new agency, no one who feels the importance of neighborhoods to the fabric of the city and to the psychology of its people. There is no one on either board who is an advocate for the city's badly organized 1.5 million tenants living under rent control. There is no one so poor as to need the use of a day care center or a municipal hospital. These new decision-makers are psychologically removed from the way ordinary people live in New York.[12]

The Municipal Assistance Corporation and the Emergency Finance Control Board were never intended, however, to be representatives of the socioeconomic makeup of the city. They were designed to improve the image of New York as a location for capital investment.

The Municipal Bond Investment Industry. The 1975 charter revision referendum provided the investment community with an excellent opportunity to display its new expertise. The new fiscal manager argued that New York needs good and innovative management. Because the city was mortgaged to long-and short-term debt obligations, obviously the lending institutions must be able to evaluate the relative effectiveness of the city management and leadership.

Municipal bonds have become big business since cities began to lose their tax base. Investors are able to make a profit by reselling bonds to the public for a higher price than they paid to the city. Syndicates, formed to purchase issues, agree to resell these at a fixed rate that will be attractive to investors. The issues are rated by various credit-rating agencies (e.g., Moody's Investors Service, Inc., Standard and Poor's, and Fitch Investor Service). Ratings are estimates of the likelihood of city repayment. The credit rating has been essentially an accountant's judgment about the relative soundness of an investment. This entails an analysis of existing debt and revenue potentials. Although investors say that they look at a city's payment records, financial structure, statistics, and state laws before making a final judgment, their basic tool is generally considered to be intuition.

In order to understand the New York City debt, it is necessary to distinguish between long-term and short-term debt. Long-term bonds are usually issued for "hardware" programs, such as capital investment. Short-term bonds provide cash to operate the government. The types of bonds are general obligaiton bonds and revenue bonds. There are also hybrids of the two basic types, such as special bonds, authority and agency bonds, and industrial-development bonds. There are three types of notes: revenue-anticipation notes (RANs), bond-anticipation notes (BANs) and tax-anticipation notes (TANs). Each of these has a different payment agreement.

An examination of the technical aspects of municipal bonds is beyond the scope of this book, but the increasing political role played by investors in city finance policy underlies the subtle shift in the priorities of government. One probable result is that investment houses will begin to hire more urban specialists so as to have their staffs able to communicate with the urban managers in fiscal and political terms.

Implicit in the fiscal analysis of a municipality are the following questions: What are the safeguards for the investors? Who determines the financial structures of the city? Is the city investment in rehabilitation and redevelopment sound? Are the pensions and salary increments in line with expected revenues? What is the city doing about employee productivity? Can the city do its job with fewer people? The people who ask these questions are not accountable to anyone except the investors, who in turn are likely to refuse a project that makes good political but dubious financial sense.

Politicians responded to these fiscal inquiries by offering more assurance, more taxes, more accountants and management personnel. In this major fiscal realignment, investors and rating services sought and received guarantees from all levels of government. Standard and Poor's, one of the flagships of the investment community, endorsed numbers 1 and 2 of the 1975 charter revision proposals in the election. These two proposals added more auditing and accounting procedures to the city's administrative structure and reduced the mayor's power in the budgetary process.

Economic Implications for Agency Personnel Policy. The uncertainties of the fiscal situation interfered with the routine staffing calculations of agency heads. Throughout the history of the city personnel system, economic problems had slowed but not permanently abated the growth of city agencies. The 1975 fiscal crisis cannot be compared to the Great Depression, but its initial phase clearly indicated that the city could no longer practice staffing as usual. The regular staffing policy of the city was to add personnel when there was money available. This policy had gone so far as to generate service demands by decentralizing service units (e.g., schools, hospitals, and neighborhood city halls). When there was no money the response was to institute a temporary hiring freeze. This policy was a reaction to the policy initiatives taken by the state and federal governments. These higher levels of government mandated new programs and new staffing patterns.

For an agency head the 1975 fiscal crisis created a new political and organizational environment. In the past staffing decisions involved three major groups. These were (1) the mayor's office staff (e.g., OMB); (2) inside constituency groups (e.g., employees, cliques, unions); and (3) outside constituency groups (e.g., reformers, clients). As a result of the 1975 fiscal crisis Group One wanted the agency heads to make staff reductions and report the statistics immediately. This group hoped to use these statistics to present their financial case to their audience (e.g., investors, Congress).

Group Two (i.e., workers and unions) wanted to retain both personnel and service levels. If this was not possible, this group preferred service cuts to personnel cuts. If personnel cuts could not be avoided, then layoffs should be made in terms of seniority. Group Two believed that a more efficiently managed organization could reduce overall costs. It also sought evidence that agency heads were making a vigorous defense against any changes in the agency mission.

Group Three (clients and reformers) desired no service changes but reductions in overall costs. This group believed that the agency heads had the power to make immediate changes. Although this group was a potential ally in the campaign to reduce the agency staffing patterns, it could not be mobilized. Instead of mobilizing Group Three, most agency heads spent their time disabusing the public of the notion that administrators possess absolute administrative powers.

The agency head had four policy choices. First, he or she could institute an attrition policy with no replacements, thereby paring the agency staff. This would satisfy Group One, alienate Group Two, and get little reaction from Group Three. The second choice was to pursue a simple replacement policy with a no-growth strategy. This would alienate Group One, satisfy Group Two, and satisfy Group Three. A no-growth policy assumed that a discontinuation of services at their present levels would not seriously threaten the city's survival, tranquility, or image. Client hardship was usually the reason not to pursue a no-growth strategy.

The third choice was a replacement and controlled growth policy. This strategy could alienate Group One, satisfy Group Two, and potentially alienate Group Three. If this strategy were adopted the agency head could make a case that continued growth was necessary because his or her agency was either saving money for the city or that changes in federal and state law mandated personnel expansion. An agency head could also argue that a status quo policy would be tantamount to severe retrenchment and reduced efficiency.

The fourth choice was to continue the old staffing patterns and pursue a confrontation strategy. This strategy would alienate Group One and Group Three. Group Two (especially the unions) were potential allies in this strategy. The strategy assumed that (1) the fiscal crisis was temporary; (2) most heads would pursue one of the other three strategies; or (3) other agencies would try to take advantage of the current uncertainty and confusion.

None of these strategies or choices was without risks and benefits. Neither could an agency head hope to satisfy all groups simultaneously. A prudent agency head would select a strategy consistent with his or her career aspirations, agency clout, and judgment. In making a choice, an agency head had also to keep in mind the reactions of the other agency heads. The wrong choice might mean losing one's job and reputation as a competent administrator. If one were to make the right choice, that might generate temporary enemies and temporary supporters. In other words, right choices do not eliminate uncertainities nor win permanent friends.

The attrition/no-growth policy, advocated by the fiscal managers, could achieve economy and deal directly with one of the causes of the fiscal crisis. An agency head pursuing such a strategy might generate understanding editorials in the media, but the strategy could generate hostility throughout the agency. The agency staff might revolt, causing administrative delay and service failures. There was also the risk that one's colleagues (other agency heads) might perceive the attrition/no-growth strategy as a sign of weakness and vacillation. Rival agency heads might pursue an expansionist strategy to collect laid-off workers, abandoned facilities, and clients. In other words, the attrition/no-growth policy which seemed rational given the exigencies of the fiscal crisis, was not without its political and organizational risks. The political risk was reduced if an agency head restricted personnel reductions to workers with little seniority and service diminutions to relatively unorganized client groups. Unfortunately, such a policy would affect the welfare poor and working poor more than it would hurt the organized middle class.

The Poor and the Unemployed. The poor and the unemployed are relatively powerless groups in any city. The 1975 fiscal realignment in New York City and its concomitant restraints on the budget were particularly painful and destabilizing for these groups. Without the leadership of an organized political group, the poor are forced to rely on the largess of other interest groups. The political arena of New York City is not kind to unorganized groups. After the demise of Tammany in the early twentieth century, the working class failed to develop a reliable grass-roots organization. Since LaGuardia, New York politics had been a middle-class reform movement, often at variance with the aspirations of the powerless.

The relatively powerless groups found that protest was no longer an effective tool because it was seen by the public as a nuisance that could safely be ignored in times of budget paring. In 1975, for example, a group of rehabilitated drug addicts held a demonstration in front of Gracie Mansion, the mayor's residence. But the event was not covered by the press with the intensity that it would have received in the 1960s. The former addicts camped out for three days until the mayor promised to review the city's decision to reduce the number of clinics operated by the Addiction Service Agency. The only problem with this was that Mayor Beame did not determine the fiscal policies of the city. The proper place to protest would have been in front of the office of the Emergency Control Board. The former addicts' leader was operating under the rules of prealignment politics.

As the fiscal crisis progressed, urban managers were able to convince the public that sacrifices had to be made everywhere. Powerless groups were unable to mount a countercampaign to protect themselves against the budget-paring rhetoric and policies of the new fiscal manager. Nor could these groups depend on their traditional political friends (i.e., the unions), who were themselves trying to assess how they would fare in the new alignment.

The cutback in city jobs particularly hurt those who had recently been added to the city payroll. The Commission on Human Rights' study of the layoff strategy of the city revealed that in contrast to white workers, who lost 22% of their number, minorities suffered far greater percentage losses. Hispanics were the hardest hit, with more than half (51.2%) of Hispanic workers separated from their jobs. Black employees lost more than a third (35%) of their positions, with black males alone suffering a 40% loss. Other minorities, a category which includes Asian Americans and American Indians were reduced by 30%.[13]

The meaning of these figures is that whites did not make a contribution to the layoff pool equal to their number in the work force. Whites represented 67 percent of the labor force but contributed only 52 percent to the layoffs. The minorities contributed 43 percent of all separations, although they represented 33 percent of the work force.

As mentioned earlier, minority jobs were concentrated in the soft-line agencies. The paraprofessional category lost 85 percent of its jobs. The clerical, service-maintenance, and paraprofessional workers made up 52.6 percent of the labor force, but accounted for 73 percent of the separations. Ten percent of the loss of paraprofessional jobs was due to the discontinuation of the Work Relief Employment Program, a program to employ welfare recipients.[14]

Pension Funds, Budget Packages, and Bargaining Politics. The history of the fiscal crisis suggests that the city-employee unions' leadership did not fully understand the city's fiscal condition. The unions, with no contingency plans, found themselves muddling through the summer of 1975 displaying makeshift political postures. Many union leaders had only partial information about the financial condition of the city. As a result, the unions suffered membership losses through attrition, and heavy blows to their credibility.

The city was threatened by the spectacle of firemen and police passing out inflammatory literature in airports and bus terminals, warning travelers of the dangers of the city's lack of sufficient public-safety personnel. There were muted references to a general strike. Health and human-services workers' unions claimed that their membership was experiencing more personnel cuts than other unions. Unions began fighting among themselves. Consequently the initial reactions of the unions to the fiscal crisis were damaging to their public image. Some public goodwill was lost. Most of this goodwill was regained when the unions allowed their pension funds to be used as part of the city budget package during the height of the fiscal crisis.

The fiscal crisis and subsequent financial realignment upset the delicate balance of relationships within the municipal-employee arena. Unions could no longer depend upon the largess of ambitious politicians as one of their major weapons in labor negotiations. Politicians assumed a tough posture toward unions in order to impress the voters and investors. Several oversight groups monitored the city's finances. Whereas politicians once had only the unions to satisfy, they now had two congressional committees, the Emergency Control Board, the Deputy State Comptroller, the Secretary of the Treasury and the President of the United States. The days of fiscal home rule for New York City were gone.

The unions responded well to the loss of political and economic clout. Their decision to invest their pension funds in city bonds was effectively publicized to attract as much public support as possible. The unions' attack on the banks was effective with the public, but did not seem to convince the banks that they should take any more risks with their investors' monies. The media gave the unions high marks for rising above petty self-interest and for delaying new contract demands.

The future of the city-employee unions held the possibility of "union cannibalism," the same kind of organizational raiding and cooptation that occurred during the unions' formative years in the 1950s. The large unions had to recover their revenue losses (membership dues), and the fastest way to achieve this would be through a merger with the small organizations.

As the city bureaucracy changed its orientation from labor-intensive to professional, supplemented by computers and other technology, the unions were forced to compete for workers in a dwindling labor market. As the state or federal government assumed control of the city's welfare service programs, the unions faced the possibility of yet another loss of influence. Greater involvement by Congress in city finances led unions to shift their attention and energy from local to congressional politics, and in the theater of politics, they had to compete with the nations' giant interest groups.

New Actors, Old Crisis. The voters reacted swiftly to the events of 1975 and the Republican party's parsimonious attitude. They voted for Democrat Jimmy Carter for President and Daniel Moynihan for senator. Unlike his predecessor James Buckley, Senator Moynihan became an elegant advocate of a federal rescue of the city. The Carter administration, after some hesitancy and political posturing by Senator William Proxmire of Wisconsin, decided to commit itself to a billion dollar loan guarantee.

The 1978 loan guarantees restored investors' confidence in city fiscal affairs. The five major public-employee pension funds began reselling MAC bonds in July 1979. In the same year Jim Ruth of Merrill Lynch Pierce Fenner and Smith was moved to comment that "the market for MAC's has improved significantly in the last six months and that is indirectly because of the city's situation improving. But I wouldn't put too optimistic a construction on this."[15] Later that year the pension funds resold MAC bonds for more than $53 million to Citibank, making a profit of $1.5 million. Indeed things were going so well that Felix Rohatyn returned to his old investment firm Lazard Freres and Company. The investment community began to renew its faith in the city's financial chances for survival.

In fiscal 1979-1980 the city was able to sell revenue anticipatory notes (RAN) to the general public through the normal Wall Street underwriter process. In that same year the city used $750 million of $1.65 million of the loan guarantee, or 45 percent of the total. The remaining $900,000 million of loan guarantees is still unresolved. The question is whether the United States Treasury will issue the guarantees. At this writing, the city has not formally requested them.

Another significant change for the city was the 1977 election of Edward I. Koch as mayor. Koch promised new leadership and a new fiscal policy. The mayor seems to have accomplished the former by shifting the media spotlight to himself. He has skillfully used humor and personalism (i.e., making personal appearances in neighborhoods and injecting his personality into the fiscal controversies.) For a time the fiscal crisis faded into the local-news section of the newspapers.

Koch then took on the establishment. He publicly criticized the $250,000 consulting contract MAC had made with Lazard Freres and Company, the investment banking firm of former MAC chairman Rohatyn. The mayor asserted, "I don't think they should give such contracts. There is something demeaning about it. It may not be a legal conflict of interest but it's certainly a moral conflict of interest."[16]

The new chairman, George Gould, former president of the Madison Fund, reacted quickly to the mayor's comments. On one occasion he accused the mayor of "meddling in MAC affairs. I feel our actions need very little justification. . . . The mayor should stick to running the city."[17] On another occasion he asserted that "the mayor does a lot of things he knows well. But I must confess I know more about finance and financial advising than he does." Gould continued, "I am not going to stand for the mayor or anybody else telling me that I or MAC have any moral conflicts. . . . I have been on Wall Street for twenty-seven years and I know who is good and who isn't."[18]

Lazard Freres and Company offered to return the contract. Gould resigned, and in a fascinating turn of events Rohatyn returned as chairman of MAC. The mayor, with this bit of theatricality, had given the fiscal managers their comeuppance and enticed the hero of the fiscal crisis to take his old job back. This was all done while reasserting a strong role for the mayor in future fiscal affairs. It was indeed a strange twist in the political theatrics of the fiscal crisis.

Meanwhile the influence of the onetime powerful Emergency Finance Control Board waned, and the "Emergency" was dropped from its title. Steven Berger resigned, and Comer S. Coppie, a former officer of the federal Office of Management and Budget, became the new executive director. Mr. Coppie took a low-key approach disclaiming any political policy-making responsibilities. Upon his appointment he asserted, "It is important for a fiscal monitor not to interfere with functions that are really city prerogatives."[19] This statement was important for symbolic reasons and reinforced Mayor Koch's attempts to assume more visibility, if not control, over the fiscal affairs of the city. It also reassured the investment community that it would not have to deal with two governments in the city—one political and one fiscal. None of these new attitudes could have been possible without the 1978 loan guarantees.

SUMMARY

Fred Ferretti, the chronicler of the New York City fiscal crisis of 1975, observed:

When the city began going broke, the accountants were called names, reviled, forced to retire with pensions. But the programs that had proliferated under them were cut, and they continued to be cut. The ultimate victims of the city's fiscal gimmickry were its citizens who found themselves without the services they had come to believe were their right, and with a bunch of businessmen in the saddle urging more and more cuts upon them, they asked why they had to suffer. And nobody could give them an answer.[20]

Reporters Jack Newfield and Paul DuBrul offered similar conclusions about the crisis:

They have done their worst to us—the banks; Nelson Rockefeller; Lindsay, Beame, Nixon, Ford, and lesser politicians; the muggers; the Sun Belt; the permanent government. Our services have been cut. Cops and firemen are unemployed. People are dying for want of a bed or a night nurse in municipal hospitals. Our children are not learning, fifty to a classroom. The upward mobility that came with a free college education is gone. Democracy is diminished.[21]

Far from being the bitter fruits of profligacy, as suggested by many congressmen, journalists, and scholars, the near fiscal collapse of New York City was positive in the sense that it signaled the end of urban financing as we know it and the emergence of a new class of political actors—the fiscal managers. In retrospect, the unfolding of the city's financial plight in a presidential election year and at a time of relatively low inflation probably saved the city from walking the fiscal plank. The new city financial plan (now extended to four years) which requires large-scale borrowing from the private sector and loan guarantees from the federal government, mandates that locally elected officials defer to the judgment of the investment experts.

The new fiscal managers differ not only in education, background, and ambition but also in temperament from their predecessors, the academic reformers. Whereas the academic reformers stressed efficiency and training for civil servants, the fiscal managers stress budgets, investment portfolios, and cooperation with the private-investment community. The managers are not interested in the day-to-day operations of the city, nor are they attempting to involve themselves in electoral politics. In order to ascend or achieve hegemony, the fiscal managers have had to discredit the old regime (the academic reformers).

Authors Newfield and DuBrul criticized the fiscal managers for appointing only financial experts to the boards and staff. The fiscal managers have partially answered this criticism by adding women, blacks, and labor representatives to the Financial Control Board and its staff. The managers have also defused the emergency atmosphere around the fiscal crisis. Nonetheless the social conditions cited by Newfield and DuBrul have not abated but rather have been accorded less press attention. Conditions have changed so much that Mayor Koch was able to close city hospitals, a feat thought impossible until recently.

The federal loan guarantee authorized under Public Law 95-339 mandated an independent audit of the city's books. This provision for review by outside certified accountants assures the fiscal managers' access to the city's books and provides the public with more independent financial information. In June 1978, the fiscal managers knew for the first time how much money the city had in the banks. They also knew the exact amount of claims against the city's revenue. One fiscal manager gleefully proclaimed, "No more Beame specials, we now have financial statements." Although the city's financial statements are not written exactly in complete accordance with generally accepted accounting principles, officials claim that they are close. If true, New York could be the most accountable city in the world.[22]

The fiscal managers have established themselves as the new reformers. Along with the status and authority comes the obligation to create good political theater. The television coverage of budget and loan hearings in Congress helped their cause.

Maintaining a good performance will be much more difficult and complex for the new fiscal managers than it was for their predecessors, the academic reformers, who started in the 1930s and had a smaller audience. There are two important changes since that time that will affect the managers' political presentation: the media coverage of events and the manner of such coverage. A unique convergence of communications technology, personality, and economic circumstance has resulted in a theater where villians and heroes must act out their parts with thespian skill.

The advent of these new managers suggests that New Yorkers have experienced a critical epoch in their city's history, one in which significant changes are being made in the way the city conducts its affairs. To interpret the changes in city administration as revolutionary may be excessive, but it is no exaggeration to say that this city has lost its autonomy in fiscal matters. New Yorkers should not lament the passing of this stage of political and economic development, however, but welcome it as the dawn of a new era in the city's history.

Since the advent of media coverage in politics, the public has come to expect politics to be entertaining. Incompetent and corrupt politicians are tolerated as long as they are not dull. If politics is not interesting enough to hold our attention, many of us simply tune it out. The issues of city government have always had trouble competing with those of the federal government for drama, excitement, and suspense. Traditionally the federal government has been able to steal the limelight from the city. Selling nuclear weapons to foreign powers, for example, makes better news than filling potholes in city streets. But clever media packaging has nonetheless made New York City's scandals and fiscal crises a number one attention getter.

The fiscal crisis of 1975 represented political theater at its best. Through efforts of the media, a problem in accounting was converted into a drama of suspense and intrigue. Mayor Beame was portrayed as a gentle old man, struggling to save New York from the clutches of steely-eyed bankers. The banking and investment community insisted that city services be reduced and layoffs be made before investing further in city bonds. The bankers demanded an ironclad guarantee for their investments from a city on the brink of bankruptcy. The mayor called the banking com munity irresponsible, and the banking community called him incompetent. The public-employee unions joined in these name-calling histrionics, and demanded salary increases and no layoffs as the price for participation in the budget preparation. They even hinted at a general strike if the city conducted massive layoffs.

All this maneuvering came directly into the homes of New Yorkers. Live and in living color, it was a parade of personalities and endless disagreements—all in all, a grand spectacle. This aspect of politics was too serious to ignore and in fact quite entertaining. Indeed, many individuals became intimately involved in these events, albeit vicariously.

The media seemed to be guiding the public carefully through the events leading to bankruptcy. Then suddenly, as it has happened so often in the movies from Tom Mix to John Wayne, the hero, in the person of Governor Carey, came to the rescue. In this media version of events, the governor was cast as an honest broker rallying to save the city from its worst enemies, the spendthrift local politicians on the one hand and the thoughtless union leaders on the other. After the state's creation of the Emergency Finance Control Board and the Municipal Assistance Corporation, the governor was able to convince investors and the public that the city was now in frugal hands. It was safe once again to invest in municipal bonds. The federal government agreed to make low-interest loans to the city, and the unions agreed to buy city bonds with their pension funds. New York was saved from bankruptcy!

As is the case with good drama, the watching public experienced a variety of emotions during the crisis. The public was confused by the jargon of the bankers and accountants, amused or disgusted by the antics of the police and fire unions. Finally it felt exhausted and relieved upon hearing the announcement that the city had been saved.

The fiscal crisis illustrates the theatrical basis of personnel politics in New York City. It shows how a municipality with over 80 percent of its budget committed to salaries and benefits can become entangled in the avarice of interest groups and the ambitions of politicians. Thus, the new fiscal managers should be prepared to move in three directions toward developing a new personel policy and management ethos: (1) toward repudiating the new patronage as a special privilege of academic reformers; (2) toward more public support for agency heads faced with more Hobson's choices; (3) toward expansion of management training programs based on the new realities of city revenues; and (4) toward an effective use of the media to explain new policies.

6

PERSONNEL POLICY
AS A REFLECTION
OF GROUP INTEREST

The staffing process is critical to the personnel enterprise. Controlling the flow of employees in and out of government is more than a necessary function of personnel management. Staffing is also a service function in that the personnel staff is responsible for the care and well-being of all employees while they remain in the government. Given the political nature of New York's Department of Personnel, it does not conform to textbook models of personnel administration, for its role is not to make personnel policy but to legitimate it. This requires both technical and political skills.

In a large urban-personnel bureaucracy, political-electoral legitimation is replaced by technocratic legitimation which refers to technical expertise but is amenable to organized group pressure. The personnel department usually responds to highly organized groups and distributes resources accordingly. Unorganized individuals, even those in ad hoc groups, are safely ignored. When approached by unorganized individuals, the personnel department has traditionally raised the merit or fiscal issue.

For organized groups the personnel department's role is to act as umpire (i.e., by rule making and interpreting). This is a difficult role since the department has no enforcement powers over outside groups. Therefore, the personnel department is powerless to protect interest groups from each other or to prevent interest groups from encroaching on its routine administrative activities (i.e., classification, testing, compensation).

The struggles over classification, testing, and compensation are not altogether battles of opposing groups and actors; rather, they are more of a fight among changing coalitions with similar interests. In employee-relations politics, there are no permanent friends, only permanent interests. To the outsider, New York City's politics seems to be in a continuous negotiating process, never able to resolve any of the city's agency and employee problems. The perennial collective-bargaining process is only the visible tip of the iceberg, which hides an abundance of deals, accommodations, and agreements. It is therefore only fair to note that survival in this environment requires shifts in priorities of organizational and political behavior at the expense of compliance with technical laws (i.e., Chapter 35 of the revised New York City Charter, 1974, and Chapter 700 of the amended New York State Civil Service Law, 1958) and regulations. It is within this context that the recruitment and selection of personnel take place.

Personnel Policy as Negotiation. The exigencies of the 1975 fiscal crisis changed the staffing calculations of most personnel interest groups. This in turn changed the behavior of the agency heads and their personnel staffs. Agency supervisors were told to refuse subordinate personnel requests that were out of line with the new agency guidelines. Agency personnel staff were told not to process requests from line supervisors which violated these mandates. Nonetheless, line supervisors have continued to receive pressure from subordinates to facilitate personnel requests (e.g., merit raises, promotion, and training leaves). Many line supervisors apply pressure to the agency personnel staff. If that does not work, line supervisors appeal to the agency commissioners. Usually such appeals trigger a series of negotiations involving line supervisors, agency heads, and agency personnel staff.

Once the requests have cleared the agency personnel staff review, they are transmitted to the city's Department of Personnel for a second review. This second review is made by a designated task force or individual within the central office. The requests are checked for form number, content, and authorizations. If there are problems, they are resolved by negotiation between the city's Department of Personnel and the agency's personnel staff.

Although most of the paperwork is done by the agency's personnel office, the city's Department of Personnel still exercises some control through request review. The administrative delay in the system can be traced to the breakdown of communication between agency staff and the city's Department of Personnel. To break the impasse, agency personnel staffs exert pressure on the city's Department of Personnel through their commissioners. The commissioners, in turn, exert pressure on the director of the city's Personnel Department. These actions then trigger another round of negotiations among the various parties.

Before the 1975 charter revision the city's personnel director was able to defend himself against the pressures of agency commissioners. At present the director's visibility and powers have been somewhat reduced, but he still retains the general supervision of civil service recruitment, examination, and classification.

There have been a number of directors of the Personnel Department since the inception of the office in 1954. The first was Joseph Schechter (1954-1959), a lawyer and former counsel to the New York State Department of Civil Service. He reorganized the department and had a reputation as a professional. He published an article in a personnel journal and achieved some national visibility. Theodore Lang (1960-1965), who had served as assistant director of personnel, also had a reputation as a professional. Solomon Hoberman (1966-1969) came up through the ranks of the civil service, but he quickly gained visibility and acquired a reputation as a professional. Harry Bronstein (1970-1973) came from the Department of Rents and Housing Maintenance. He gained a reputation as the civil servants' civil servant. Alphonse D'Ambrose (1974-1975), who was a lawyer and former counsel to the city's Department of Personnel, gained a reputation as a civil servant. Thomas Roche (1975-1979) came to the department from the mayor's executive staff; although he had been a civil servant, he gained a reputation as a politician. S. Michael Nadel (1979-1981), a lawyer, came to the department from the governor's executive staff; he gained a reputation as a politician.

The directors who gained professional reputation combined technical skills with open creative talent. The first personnel directors—Joseph Schechter and Theodore Lang—wrote extensively on city personnel policy. They, along with Solomon Hoberman, were respected by the academic community and the reformers. Under Schechter, Lang, and Hoberman, the department enjoyed a professional reputation. All three directors were oriented toward change and expansion in the department. They were also blessed with strong support from their mayors.

A tidy systematic person would find the office of city personnel director frustrating. Coping with the chaos of the personnel system and being the handmaiden of the entire city bureaucracy requires flexibility and openness. Not only does the personnel director have the mayor—and his budget director—looking over his shoulders, but he also has agency heads and union staff maligning his competence. If this is not enough, he has the courts trying to do his job for him, overruling his regulations, and leaving him with legal mandates he cannot fulfill. Of all the actors in the personnel drama, the personnel director receives the fewest kudos for his efforts. He is often ignored by powerful labor leaders, upstaged by ambitious mayors, and belittled by the press and the academic community.

The impotence of the personnel director was exacerbated by the 1975 charter revision. (The changes in the charter have been discussed in detail in Chapter 3.) The personnel director is no longer a match for agency heads. Thus the great personnel innovator of the 1950s is now the chief clerk in the 1980s.

The strides toward a strong personnel director slowed when mayors started recruiting persons who regarded the job as an enforcement office. Such persons gained reputations as civil servants' civil servants. The tone of the department changed as its personnel increasingly saw themselves as clerks. Suspicious and protective, the members of the staff became rule-enforcement oriented and very specialized in an effort to isolate themselves from the political leadership. This rigid environment may have contributed to the stagnation of the department before the fiscal crisis. During the crisis, the department had no systematic attrition or manpower policy: it could not even provide the beleaguered Mayor Beame with meaningful statistics about manpower in city agencies. Finally, the mayor removed the personnel director and eventually assigned from his staff Thomas Roche to head the department.

Mr. Roche was a political personnel director and made no pretense about having technical skills. Usually such individuals are relatively well adapted to the political environment of personnel policy. Mr. Roche did his job so well that he was retained by the incoming Koch administration. The present director, S. Michael Nadel, also came from the political ranks.

There have undoubtedly been more leadership styles and combinations, but the job has never lived up to its potential. This is partly because the reformers could not agree on the nature of the role of the director. Some wanted the director's role strengthened; others wanted to make it more amenable to the mayoral directions. The latter group seems to have won in the latest round of charter revision. Agency heads may have won a battle, but the war over position classification, compensation, and selection will probably continue. If it does, then the city personnel director may gain a reputation as a good negotiator.

The director of the Office of Management and Budget, on the other hand, wants to build a reputation as a personnel cutter. Wallace Sayre and Herbert Kaufman's description of the budget director in the 1950s still applies to the present-day director. They described the job as "one of austerity without drama, of influence gained through an infinite attention to detail rather than to broad policy, of power exercised to preserve the *status quo* rather than in behalf of innovation, of maintaining the precarious balance of the city's revenues, and expectations of both the service-demanding and money-providing forces in the city's political process."[1]

The 1975 fiscal crisis changed the nature of the budget director's job, expanding his audience from the quiet Board of Estimate to noisy center stage in the continuing drama of competing interest groups. Has the job of budget director remained a "prescription for unpopularity," as characterized by Sayre and Kaufman? Although the fiscal crisis made the office very popular in the minds of the investment community, it did not make the budget director's name a household word.

Before the period of fiscal crisis, the budget director had been able to create a quasi-personnel department within his office. Using his role on the Board of Estimate, he could overrule, offset, or delay decisions made by the personnel director or heads of agencies. Sayre and Kaufman summarized the situation: "The personnel director proposes and the budget director disposes."[2]

The 1975 charter revision, which severely reduced the budget director's role in the making of personnel policy, strengthened his role as the mayor's chief fiscal lobbyist. The director had to convince both the Board of Estimate and the City Council of the soundness and conciseness of the mayor's budget. Defense of the budget became more difficult because the City Council housed its budget experts in the newly established Legislative Office of Budget Review. In addition, hundreds of financial experts from Congress, the New York State government, and the investment community annually combed the city budget for discrepancies.

Many of these discrepancies had been caused by an inefficient personnel system. There were discrepancies between the city's Department of Personnel's espoused principles of administration and those methods in actual practice. The gap was particularly apparent in traditional personnel functions.

Manpower Planning. New York City is not nearly so advanced in manpower planning as it is in planning for streets, housing, and transportation. Although the city employs thousands of people, it does not have any long-range contingency plans for new hiring, layoffs, or sudden shifts in the work force. Its planning includes the next fiscal year only. The 1975 fiscal crisis forced the city for the first time to include figures for staff reductions and attrition in its reports to Congress and to the Emergency Financial Control Board. This is as close as the city has ever come to manpower planning. For it still employs the same political calculations as it did in the nineteenth century (i.e., expand personnel to accommodate service demands arising in affluent times and cut personnel in tough fiscal times).

The largest city in the nation has no systematic way to regulate staff inadequacies, fiscal retrenchment, and internal shifts of staff between departments. Without manpower planning, it reacts to, rather than anticipating, changes in the political and economic environment. Changes in mayors can trigger changes of emphasis within departments. Technology can create new jobs, shrink old ones, and enlarge others. A new law can change the way an agency operates. A public demand for more accountability can divert agency resources to program evaluation units. Since there is no planning, departments operate by a "norm of funding": as just noted, their staffs expand when there are funds in the budget, and losses are not replaced when there is less money available.

Publicity and the Great Job Rush. Unlike most cities, New York has always enjoyed a large pool of qualified and enthusiastic job seekers. In 1973 the announced openings for sanitation workers brought out 80,000 to 90,000 examination takers. A record number of applicants (160,000) filed with the Department of Personnel. When police entrance examinations were held the following year, almost 60,000 individuals scrambled for less than 500 job openings. Why? Because the city had achieved working conditions that were competitive with the private sector (e.g., high pay, fringe benefits, and strong union contracts). The job rush was slowed down, however, by the fiscal crisis of 1975. During the crisis the Department of Personnel denied its reputation as being a cornucopia of jobs, and was given the thankless task of informing employees of pending layoffs and telling applicants of job freezes.

Before the fiscal crisis, the target of the recruitment program was primarily the civil service community, which was composed of approximately 500,000 civil service employees who worked for the city, state, and federal governments. It was indeed a community within a community, with two weekly newspapers and a social network that would rival some small towns.

The *Chief,* a publication established in 1897 by Frank Prial, provided this community with the latest information about job openings, benefits, and civil service laws and regulations. The *Civil Service Leader,* a tabloid that described itself as "America's largest newspaper for public employees," boasted of a circulation of 250,000. When city departments desired to reach the civil service community, they did so through these weeklies. Recently the *Civil Service Leader* was taken over and merged with the *Chief.*

Communicating with the general public required placing announcements in the regular daily papers, posting signs in public buildings, and placing advertisements with employment agencies. Such a publicity effort, small in scope and budget, was able to generate thousands of applicants. Table 6.1 shows the number of examinations administered by New York departments and the number of applications received for selected years.

The gaps in this data reflect poor statistical record keeping in the Department of Personnel, not the present writer's personal choice of years. The lack of emphasis on statistics also reflects the lack of manpower planning by this agency. Without data general administrative planning is difficult if not impossible. Nonetheless reformers continue to force-feed professionalism and productivity to the Department of Personnel.

TABLE 6.1: Number of Examinations and Applications
in Selected Years

Year	Number of Examinations	Number of Applications
1951	324	116,467
1952	322	101,174
1954	308	61,827
1957	285	122,118
1958	241	70,818
1959	257	94,034
1961	313	124,385
1963	301	211,000
1964	291	141,000
1968	510	196,500
1972	634	233,598

Source: Department of Personnel, Annual Reports.

The Search for Respectability. As we suggested in Chapter 2, the struggle in city politics was concerned with proving that the present system was somewhat better than the old one of Tammany Hall. Thus, personnel politicians were constantly searching for ways to demonstrate progress. High-ranking civil servants were also recruited to defend the new system and attack the old spoils system. Legitimizing the new spoils system has been an uphill battle, but the reformers in government were able to show a measurable difference between the new personnel administration and the old partisan one. (Some of the changes advocated and implemented by reformers have already been outlined in the previous chapter.)

New York City first adopted position classification during the Mitchel administration. The mayor and his efficiency experts attempted to reorganize the city workers along "scientific-management" principles. Robert Moses did the first detailed analysis of titles and duties to determine the content and necessary skills for each position. After Chicago (1905), New York was the second major city to conduct such a study. This is not to say that it had not conducted internal and informal studies about positions in government before then. Indeed, during the first years of the Civil Service Commission, attempts had been made to separate, analyze, eliminate, and classify positions. The genteel reformers—unlike their successors, the academic reformers—did not insist on dissecting each job into its smallest unit. Their efforts were geared toward the elimination of overlapping and duplicate jobs.

Emphasizing the Benefits. In order to convince the public that the city's personnel policies had come a long way since the days of the Edson administration, the Personnel Department adopted a policy of saturating the city-operating agencies with position-classification plans, salary and pay plans, and training programs. Even consultants like personnel experts Griffenhagen and Associates appeared on the scene, attempting to apply a set of principles to the city classification plan.[3] They also stressed the positive benefits of classification plans:

A position-classification plan establishes a uniform occupational terminology; serves as a base for an equitable and logical pay plan; facilitates the preparation of informative budgets for personnel services; serves as a foundation for the recruiting, testing, and certification activities of the central personnel agency; clarifies promotion and transfer transactions; aids in planning, classifying, and improving organization; facilitates the development of good employee-management relations; makes it possible to compile meaningful personnel statistics; and in general tends to systematize and facilitate the determination and execution of many types of personnel policies and specific personnel or pay transactions.[4]

Professor O. Glenn Stahl would probably agree with this characterization. He has asserted that "neither a financial nor a personnel agency can properly perform functions unless there are titles and definitions.[5] Professor Stahl is correct if one accepts the notion that a city department of personnel is a regulatory agency. In New York City, the Department of Personnel did not play an umpire role but rather a bookkeeping or clerical one. Position-classification decisions were usually made in negotiations between the operating agency, budget director, and the unions. The reason for this was that the very act of defining positions was a political one. No amount of technical imperatives or administrative requirements could take position classification out of the political arena.

Although Stahl and other scholars of personnel administration advocated separating position classification from compensation, the linkage was fused by the unionization of public employment. Public employees were and are interested in upgrading their salaries in the process of retitling themselves.

During the Joseph Schechter tenure as personnel director, the Career and Salary Plan, a modern classification plan, was introduced. The new plan was imposed upon the old classification plan. The old plan was less systematic and allowed employees to move up the promotional

**TABLE 6.2: City Employees in the Classified and Unclassified Services
1904–1934
(selected years)**

	Unclassified	Exempt	Competitive	Noncompetitive	Labor	Total
1904	256	669	19,786	3,784	12,343	33,017
1909	251	716	30,184	5,159	18,696	54,965
1910	247	729	28,873	4,826	18,303	52,478
1913	273	782	31,003	5,411	17,905	55,574
1914	267	805	30,898	5,813	17,737	55,570
1918	256	738	30,698	6,479	15,958	54,129
1925	249	915	41,638	8,334	19,522	70,658
1926	249	914	44,180	9,367	19,098	73,808
1932	229	899	53,132	11,049	25,512	89,400
1934	390	619	46,699	15,035	23,309	86,364

Source: Verticle File, Municipal Reference Library.

ladder quickly. Many workers opposed the new plan which required promotional examinations. They took their case to court, and the court ruled that employees hired before the imposition of the new plan could continue to get promoted under the old plan. This resulted in a personnel system with two classification plans and two separate promotion requirements. By 1975, most of the old-plan employees had left the personnel system, but this incident demonstrates the difficulties that faced reform directors in the Personnel Department.

Mayors found position-classification to be a tool for facilitating patronage and eliminating political appointees from the previous administration. The Mitchel administration and its successors used the

**TABLE 6.3: Exempt Class as Percentage
of Total Employment, 1932–1962**

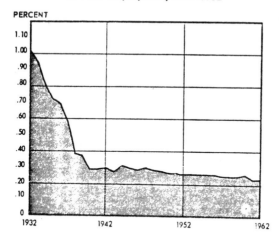

Source: Annual Report of Department of Personnel,
1963, p. 19.

**TABLE 6.4: Number of Employees in Classified Service
1902–1962**

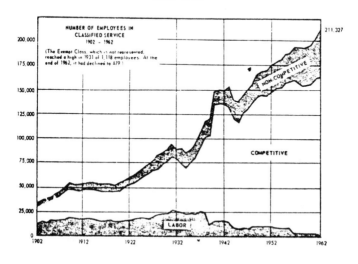

Source: Annual Report of Department of Personnel,
1963, p. 19.

classification goals to reform the personnel system. William Brown, Mayor LaGuardia's political biographer, believed that much of the success of LaGuardia's civil service reforms was achieved through the use of the classification system. LaGuardia was able to eliminate exempt categories and reduce the opportunities for patronage. Table 6.2 shows where classified service employees were in the first years of the LaGuardia administration.

Table 6.2 also shows a trend away from nonclassified or exempt positions and toward classified ones. This change in the recruitment pattern facilitated the demise of party influence in the bureaucracy. Mayor Wagner discovered that he no longer needed the support of the regular Democratic party, and decided to reject the organization's first reelection bid. Tables 6.3 and 6.4 show the continuing decline of the exempt and labor classes.

Despite these trends, most of the civil service studies and press reports criticized classification systems. When one reads the findings of Mayor O'Dwyer's Committee on Management Survey, one finds a repetition of standard personnel and classification jargon. The words and phrases used and the classification plans found in this survey give the impression that the civil service could be reformed simply by making clerical changes. These analysts also seemed to believe that using certain magic words would make the difference. The words that reflected a negative record were *fragmentation, overlapping, duplication, costly, uncoordinated, stagnate, delay, confusing,* and *patronage.* The words that conveyed the opposite impression were *standardized, merit, control, management, open, speed, planning, efficiency, effective,* and *training.* The classification plans developed by experts for the city usually started with a description of extant systems using the bad words and ending with recommendations described in the more positive terminology. The plans consistently recommended that the mayor—the developer's benefactor—be granted more authority over personnel matters. Regardless of the criticisms, the authors of procedural reform seldom attacked the interest group within the arena of personnel politics. Instead, they created the illusion that change was possible and that it had now been accomplished by the production of a written plan. They reinforced the illusion by remaining silent after it became obvious that little if any change had been made. The system worked as the old spoils system had; after the authors of the study have been paid, silence was in order; otherwise they might not be asked to do another plan. The new spoilsmen may not have made an art out of paying off consultants, but they certainly made it legal and respectable.

Classification as Negotiation. The New York City Personnel Department had a corps of dedicated men and women whose role in personnel politics became reduced to a level slightly above that of clerks. These men and women constantly demonstrated their usefulness to the city's politicians. As we have seen the Personnel Department had its decision-making responsibility taken over by the unions and the mayor's Office of Municipal Labor Relations. The Personnel Department, however, was still able to rewrite in personnel language decisions made in the course of labor negotiations. Furthermore, the department was still able to delay the personnel process, although even this power was subject to the largess of the big power brokers. A good example of such political delay was the department's reaction to a title request by the then newly created Consumer Affairs Department.

Phillip Schrag, the deputy commissioner of the agency, which was created in 1969, wanted to be able to make professional appointments that were noncompetitive and exempt from civil service examinations; otherwise, he would have had to hire lawyers from the civil service list. (Under the standards of grand patronage, this type of behavior is permissible because people with demonstrated talent should not be bothered with the nuisance of testing and the delay of the personnel system.) In his book, *Counsel to the Deceived,* Schrag argued that the lawyers on the civil service list "were unlikely to have the motivation I [Schrag] was seeking."[6]

Schrag tried to confuse the civil service regulating system with new titles and a separate job for each new lawyer. This was a violation of the city bureaucracy maxim against unspecified lateral entrance, which restricted upward mobility for regular members of the civil service. Herbert Schwartz, an official in the city Personnel Department, saw through Schrag's scheme and called the new lawyers a "buncha clowns."[7] Schwartz asserted that "we don't want people with no equity in the pension fund. We want people who build up ten, fifteen years equity. . . . A man with ten years' equity in the pension fund doesn't put his hand in the till, 'cause he can lose his pension rights. . . . Everyone near the till is a potential thief. . . . That's why we have civil service. We lock 'em in: they have to stay with the city forever."[8]

Schwartz was initiating Commissioner Schrag into the rites of classifying positions: It would not be in the interests of the personnel department to create jobs for which present career service workers were unable to apply. The principle of the common examination must be upheld to assure unrestricted mobility. Allowing people with a limited interest in the city service to engage in a revolving-door process would undermine the position of the Personnel Department in the employee-relations area.

Schwartz may also have known that the administration people in the Consumer Affairs Department (CAD) were using their personnel titles designated for weights-and-measures inspectors for other purposes. The misuse of existing personnel titles was an old bureaucratic trick, but the CAD administration's attack on the entire examination procedure was considered the highest form of heresy. Schrag's interpretation of the meeting between Schwartz and himself shows how outsiders failed to understand the workings of the city's personnel bureaucracy:

We came from the meeting with half a loaf. The lawyers would not be classified as "attorneys," so they would not be chosen from the same list as all other lawyers who work for the city, but only three titles would be created for the division—"Consumer Specialist" for the college-educated investigators, "Senior Consumer Specialists" for the lawyers, and for myself probably the most exotic official civil service title is the city's "Consumer Advocate." Some day, tests would be written for these positions, but we would be consulted on what types of questions would be asked. In this case, the snail's pace of the city's bureaucracy worked to our advantage; a year and a half later no one had even begun to design a test, and the Commissioner was still free to hire at will.[9]

Schrag's experience with the New York City civil service could be described as a quarter of a loaf, but he was able to get jobs for his Columbia University students. He had, however, to agree to civil service rules for the recruitment of future lawyers. Schrag's later remarks support this point. He observed that some day, when tests were to be written for those positions, he would be consulted about the kinds of questions to be asked. In other words, the personnel officer maintained the integrity of the recruitment while appearing to negotiate with Schrag and the CAD.

The Schrag case shows that the Department of Personnel's influence could be exercised before a position was institutionalized or formalized. The process of creating position specifications involved bargaining between the agency and the Personnel Department. A member of the Personnel Department could be a power broker for a week and then be reduced to being a clerk. For such an individual, delay meant maintaining the illusion of power. Delay in release of regulations was, in this sense, a power-conserving tactic within the agency.

Despite the loss of decision-making power, the staff of the Personnel Department continued to perform an important legitimizing and book-keeping function. Commissioners may not have had to clear patronage through the agency, but they needed approval to make the grand patronage appointments look respectable. With the provisional appointments removed, the Personnel Department would have little leverage with the commissioners. In addition, the department also had a statistical function, which it poorly performed.[10] Many outsiders found it incredible that heads of divisions were totally unaware of the actual numbers of city employees and their general rate of compensation.

Personnel technicians hoarded information as a defense against periodic raids by politicians and as a commodity of exchange to use in their daily intradepartmental activities. Commissioners or locally elected officials may often have told malicious stories about the people in personnel. Nevertheless, the victims of such tales have usually seemed good-natured about them, and few workers wanted to have the central personnel staff dispersed, decentralized, or shifted to the operating agencies.

Examination and Selection. In the early 1880s, Tammany Hall introduced written tests for employment in the Parks Department. By 1884, reformers had made the written test a requirement for most city jobs. The early reformers were fascinated by the magic of weeding out the incompetent and preventing the selection of embarrassing recruitment choices. The reformers' faith in testing was also attributable in part to the fact that its scoring was so amenable to quantitative analysis.

The academic reformers and researchers' desire to develop a scientific personnel administration has led to an endless search for the "right" techniques. Using the medieval science of alchemy as an analogue, researchers may be described as having sought to transform base metal (written tests) into gold (a reliable and culture-free selection mechanism). In this search, they have so far failed. There is little evidence that civil service tests predict job performance or even measure job skills. Some researchers have resigned themselves to the fact that value-free examinations are impossible.

If the verdict on testing as a selective technique is so negative, then why is it used so often and with so much confidence? Part of the answer to this question lies in the idea of the test as an initiation ordeal. The myth maintains that testing quickly eliminates misfits, below-average applicants, incompetents, the nervous and the fakers. But in reality, testing sometimes protects and promotes the very people its supporters seek to eliminate. Nevertheless, the true believers of testing continue to hold that the problem is one of refinement. They believe that in time and with more research the examinations can effectively screen out all undesirables. The search continues for the philosophers' touchstone.

Everett Wheeler, who wrote the first civil service regulations and who was a true believer in testing, was searching for such a standard when he asked a Chinese prince the secret of his nation's famous civil service. The prince replied:

It is important to pay your officials an adequate salary, otherwise they will be tempted to peculation. It is also important to send officials to serve in some province other than that of their birth. We find a great temptation in one's native province to discriminate in favor of personal friends.[11]

The remark apparently surprised Wheeler because it suggested that the Chinese had not forsaken the goals of an efficient civil service for a reliable recruitment method. Wheeler and his colleagues persisted in their belief that examinations would result in an exemplary civil service. Robert Moses's 1914 dissertation was the first serious attack on this notion. The Mitchel Administration, acting on this advice of Moses and other academic reformers, began eliminating examinations for high-level civil service positions.

Wallace Sayre, after serving as a civil service commissioner in the LaGuardia Administration, took the Moses position and also attacked excessive dependency on examinations. In a famous article he lamented the triumph of "technique over purpose" in public administration.[12] Professor Sayre noted that written examinations were limited in that they provided merely the appearance, not the substance, of measuring competency. He argued that the variables of personnel administration were too numerous and subtle to be contained within a purely statistical frame of reference. In his *Personnel Administration in the Government of New York City*, written with Herbert Kaufman, Sayre condemned the highly-routine and unimaginative process within the city's personnel-selection system.[13]

In 1973, Professors E. E. Savas and Sigmund Ginsburg found that civil service examinations had become a political tool of bureaucrats, who used the examinations to delay and deny appointments, regardless of the individual scores and rankings. The delay between examination and date of appointment allows bureaucrats to accommodate to the political wishes of the agency heads. In other words, there is no certainty that a score that places one in the top three will result in a job, or that someone with a lower score will not be selected. The "rule of three," which requires that municipal civil service personnel be selected from the three highest scorers, does not prevent the employing bureaucrat from using his or her political judgment when the occasion demands flexibility.

The enormous flexibility in the selection of candidates is particularly evident in the recruitment of the permanent senior civil service. The recruitment of civil service managers is marked by nepotism, favoritism, and petty politics. To understand fully the process, we must review the literature on political recruitment.

RECRUITMENT OF CIVIL SERVICE MANAGERS

Most forms of political recruitment are biased in favor of the current leadership group (in terms of social class, race, and sex), and restrict the roles played by other groups. The selection process of civil service managers is a commentary on group relations within a given agency. An individual candidate for a managerial position is the standard bearer for his particular ethnic group, and he is selected as representative of that group. In other words, one's ethnicity rather than one's talent is important in city departments. Within this context, the applicant for a leadership role must be socialized according to organizational norms.

The common element in the socialization of organization managers is the recognition that managing a city department requires technical expertise as well as political skill. The successful candidates must be acceptable to the internal and external clientele groups. The present discussion of civil service recruitment has profited from the theoretical literature developed by other writers on the subject.

Group Theory of Political Recruitment. For social scientists who consider themselves group theorists, society is divided into the rulers and the ruled, the activists and the apathetics, the few and the many, the leaders and the followers. Such theorists believe that these group relationships form the natural alignment of human interaction. Group leadership is a function of collective action, and hence it is found in all forms of social activity. It is through groups that individuals make claims on the general society. Groups that are successful in the struggle for resources are those with committed members, cohesion, financial resources, and good leadership. The leaders of political groups are carefully screened through candidate mechanisms. Professor Seligman has divided the selection process into five parts: (1) identification and certification of political activists; (2) sponsorship by political parties, interest groups, or agencies; (3) establishment of mobility requirements; (4) selection for roles; (5) assignment to positions.[14] For Seligman, recruitment is a winnowing process involving a conscious effort to sponsor, co-opt and draft attractive individuals. The only exception to this pattern are the self-starters who assert themselves on the political scene. Although these individuals start alone, they may be joined or co-opted by sponsors.

Although Seligman's work deals primarily with legislators and other elected officers, the model is relevant to the present discussion of civil service managers. Our organization activists are similar to Seligman's political ones. An individual interested in becoming a managerial candidate must make himself known to those who are in a position to make leadership choices. Professor Glickman has argued that after an individual has achieved visibility, he can facilitate the "take off" period of his career.[15] After achieving visibility, the candidate attracts sponsors. Professor Melvin Dalton has called these sponsoring groups cliques:

Vertical cliques can be broken down to vertical *symbiotic* and vertical *parasitic,* and horizontal to horizontal *aggressive* and horizontal *defensive* cliques. Vertical cliques usually occur in a single department. The tie is between the top officer and some of his subordinates. It is vertical in the sense that it is an up-and-down alliance between formal unequals. It could be represented as a rectangle with the altitude greater than the base. Horizontal cliques, on the other hand, cut across more than one department and embrace formal equals for the most part. The horizontal clique can be symbolized as a rectangle with a base greater than its altitude.[16]

In the current study of New York City civil service managers, many such cliques were found within the various agencies, mostly vertical and symbiotic in nature. The existence of such informal or "affinity groups" was crucial to the leadership selection process, which may be described as a system of sponsorship and socialization. These groups represent the primary sources for new managers for city departments. Because these affinity groups are also a major source of information within the agencies, they can control new applicants by withholding the necessary organizational information required for career development within the city system.

Most of these groups are based on social class, sex, race, and ethnicity. If a person is interested in a managerial career, he is admitted into an existing affinity group and socialized according to its norms; once he has met his group's requirements. David Rogers hinted about the existence of such groups in his study of the Lindsay administration. He saw them as contributing to what he called "pluralism gone wild," and he described them as follows:

The power of these groups is manifested in a variety of ways. Under the protective facade of "professionalism," they control entry into their agencies, and through civil service are able to limit the access of "outsiders." Particular agencies and civil service groups become the centers of ethnic power, despite the existence of a merit system. Thus, in New York City, the Irish dominate the police and fire departments, the Italians, the sanitation department, and the Jews, the school system and welfare agencies.[17]

Rogers believed that the existence of such divisions makes the management of the city's individual departments extremely difficult. On the other hand, the groups are important for social integration within the agencies and perform many recruiting and socializing functions for the city government. If such groups did not exist, the city would have to depend on more formalized recruitment, communication, and socialization systems.

The problem with affinity groups and cliques is that they tend to restrict the advancement and careers of nonmembers. Because blacks and Puerto Ricans are underrepresented in the cliques, it seems as if these groups were engaged in racial and ethnic discrimination. Indeed, there is underrepresentation of blacks and Puerto Ricans within the managerial stratum in all areas, but this is a result of the informal authority of the existing groups within the recruitment process, as well as their relative strength and age. Older groups are the gatekeepers in the pathway to managerial positions. They consciously and unconsciously seek people like themselves for the continuation of the "old boy" network of selection. By converting recruitment into a self-perpetuating process, affinity groups remove the risks and the uncertainty of random choice, and at the same time they insure the continuation of specific agency policies.

Outsiders and minority-group members operate at a distinct disadvantage if they want visibility and sponsorship within city departments. Ambitious blacks and Puerto Ricans do not have strong affinity groups at their disposal; consequently, they seek membership with those of other ethnic groups or cliques. This lack of group cohesion among minorities may be traced to the racial and ethnic discrimination practiced against them by society in general. The problem is compounded by the minorities' personal fears that creation of exclusive groups may be misinterpreted by the white leadership of the city agencies.

Despite the strategies of minority managers, their numbers remain small. This was quite evident in a random survey of 226 managers. Table 6.5 shows a statistical profile of a typical civil service manager.[18] In the survey, civil service managers were asked about charges that they had been helped by affinity groups and sponsors. Of the 226 managers responding, 61.1 percent identified themselves as self-starters. They cited their own abilities as the reason for their upward mobility. Another 16.1 percent believed that their success was a matter of ability and luck. They claimed "to have been in the right place at the right time." The survey did find 10 percent who confessed to having had sponsorship and assistance. The remaining 12.8 percent contains idiosyncratic answers and were recorded as "others."

TABLE 6.5: A Profile of the Managerial Pay Plan Civil Servant

Live in the city	76.0%
White	95.0%
Male	89.0%
Born in New York	76.0%
More than 50 years old	46.2%
College graduates with at least one advanced degree	41.3%
CUNY attendees	42.5%
More than 20 years of municipal service	67.5%
Started at the clerical level	18.6%
Worked in more than one bureau	45.0%
Four years or less in one position	55.7%
Persons with relatives in the Civil Service	45.5%
Supervising more than 51 workers	46.6%
Planning to retire from service	85.7%

The denials of sponsorship are not surprising because admission of membership in a clique or even acknowledgment of sponsorship would undermine the myth of the merit system of promotion. As a civil servant reported, "Sure there is an 'old boy' network, just like there is in any type of work. You can get promoted to a certain point without connections, but for the big move you need help. If you know the right people you can become a deputy commissioner."[19] The "right people" serve as gatekeepers to promotion. It is easy to look favorably on applicants who share one's views and social background. Prewitt believes that, because of time and other pressures, persons already in leadership make use of "shortcuts" when choosing new leadership.[20]

The civil service recruiting staff tends to rely on the judgment of cliques. A good recommendation from the organizational cliques is assumed to be equal to skill and dependability. The selection process is subtle and difficult to trace, but the selection of new members to the civil service seems to follow a specific pattern. Newly recruited civil service members and persons with the power to recruit tend to have the same social background.

Compensation. Career development, efficiency, and productivity may be important to students of personnel systems, but the most talked-about and controversial issue raised in the interviews conducted for this book involved salaries and wages. Many public employees believe that they are underpaid, and they seek to change this situation by applying pressure on union leaders, city councils, and state legislators. Because such tactics have worked, the notion is reinforced that not only does money exist somewhere, but also that one only has to press the right button in order to cash in.

Career public servants compare themselves to their counterparts in the private sector. They do not accept the philosophical notion that they are "special workers" who are "separate" from the competitive market. To quote a civil servant: "I may not be in the competitive market, but I am in the supermarket. I have to pay the same prices for food as the next guy, and until and unless they make special prices for us (city workers), I want the prevailing wages."[21] The unions have made their case in regard to getting good wage and benefit packages from the city. As long as the unions can deliver, they will continue to get support from the workers.

The construction of pay scales and schedules predates civil service reform. The current pay scale for classified workers has thirty-two salary grades. The salary range for Grade One is $2,250 to $3,150, and the range for grade thirty-two is $13,100 and up.[22] This pay scale was designed (1) to establish fixed wages vertically and horizontally (i.e., ranges up and down); (2) to link pay grade and job task to positional class; (3) to keep employees aware of the ranges of salaries; and (4) to insure efficiency in administration.

Compensation policies are the result of numerous management studies and labor negotiations. However, the purpose of wage scales has changed since the advent of the efficiency movement. The success of the efficiency movement in New York brought more public attention to the salaries of city workers. The movement advocated better pay for workers and emphasis on a carefully designed compensation plan. The reformers believed that a well-paid worker would produce more. History has not proved this proposition correct. The concern for adequate wages is now shared by both academic reformers and unions. Both have worked to improve wages and benefits for workers.

As is the case with classification systems, compensation plans frequently break down. The bureaucracy in New York is filled with stories of overpayment, underpayment, and computer malfunctioning. Occupational jealousy is rampant. The police believe that they should make more than those in the fire and sanitation departments. Social workers believe that they should earn more than clerical workers; yet workers (e.g., sanitation and police) who can cause serious inconvenience to the public by striking usually get the best wage settlements. It is ironic that despite New York's reputation for militant union workers, employee salaries are not substantially higher than those of uniformed workers in other cities. For example, the *New York Times* reported census data that shows New York uniformed employees were not the highest paid in the nation. Los Angeles and Detroit paid their police and firefighters higher salaries. Washington, D.C.'s sanitation workers had higher compensation ranges than their New York City counterparts.[23]

Transfers, Promotions, and Layoffs. Unlike the private sector, government bureaucracy has never been good at shifting workers where need is demonstrated, or at facilitating personnel changes that are in the interests of both the employee and the agency. The result is an oversupply of certain skills and titles in one agency and an undersupply in another. Because the city personnel system is large and unionized, wholesale transfers of employees are difficult if not impossible. In the survey discussed earlier in this chapter, little horizontal mobility (movement from one agency to another) was found among civil service managers, but considerable vertical mobility (movement up the ranks within agencies) was observed. Part of the reason for the lack of horizontal mobility is internal bureaucratic politics, which makes it essential for an individual to remain in one agency. This lack of movement has resulted in a very narrowly trained managerial force at the top.

The city has attempted to improve the management group by a pliant promotion system which rewards productivity, initiative, and talent. Quick promotions have become both a bane and a boon. The city has been able to promote young persons faster, to use quick promotions as a recruitment device, and to reward outstanding workers. Quick promotions are a bane in that they facilitate and perpetuate favoritism, nepotism, and racism.

This system of promotion is not without its critics. The unions claim that promotions should be based on scores on examinations and seniority.

The employees resent performance evaluations by supervisors because they are influenced by personality conflicts. Reformers want the system open to outsiders with higher education requirements in management for those assuming supervisory responsibilities. The court wants promotion examinations to be job-related and culture-free. In all cases the promotion system remains a part of the political process.

Layoffs are a different matter, as they have become the hobgoblin of the fiscal crisis afflicting the city. Employees generally fear discrimination in layoff processes. Youths, blacks, and women fear the seniority system. Welfare and education workers fear that city priorities favor public-safety workers. Although union contracts govern the method of layoff and recall, there is no way a contract can protect a worker from planned attrition (i.e., not replacing vacancies) or the discontinuation of an agency. The unions have also shown a tendency to negotiate a small work force and accept layoffs according to seniority. Massive layoffs are rare, but such actions may loom in the future, resulting from declining population (especially in schools), advanced technology, and financial difficulties. As one agency head put it, "The budget people do not make a big wound; they make a small one and let you bleed to death."

Grievances and Discipline. Discipline has become the most difficult problem facing the city's personnel system. It is much easier to define the offenses than to enforce discipline. New York has rules against fraud, absenteeism, insubordination, and so forth, but unionization has made prosecution and conviction difficult. Disciplinary action must be documented by a supervisor, employees notified, and appeals made available to the Civil Service Commission. This aspect of employee relations is replete with work rules and lawyers as city jobs become valuable. The multi-appeal mechanisms make it difficult and costly, in terms of time and energy, for supervisors to use the system. Disciplining professional workers is even more cumbersome because judging their level of inefficiency, incompetence, and insubordination is also problematical and hard to document. For some employees it is difficult to know where professional prerogatives begin and personality conflicts end in the supervisory-subordinate dynamic.

Despite the formalization of work rules in the early history of the municipal personnel system, controlling and inspiring employees remains difficult. Academic reformers believed that monetary incentives would induce conformity while their predecessors relied on normative incentives. Neither strategy has generated much commitment toward rules and formalized punishments and rewards. Yet employees still violate rules, present disciplinary problems, and commit unlawful acts. The civil service rules protect against arbitrary dismissal and provide for appeals procedures.

In New York City, the grievance procedure is governed by Sections 75 and 76 of the state civil service law.[24] Section 75 covers municipal employees and authorizes a formal hearing and right to counsel. Section 76 outlines the appeals procedure. An employee may appeal a verdict to the municipal civil service appeal system or to the courts. In other words, employees can elect an alternative to grievance procedures established by collective bargaining or submit to the Office of Collective Bargaining (OCB). The grievance-arbitration system is analogous to the procedures followed in the private sector. If the result of the informal hearing or conference (which is designated by the agency head) is unsatisfactory, the complaint can be submitted to the director of Municipal Labor Relations. If the employee is still dissatisfied, he can submit his problem to the OCB. The findings of arbitration are final and binding. Arbitration seeks to apply the language of contracts in the light of unanticipated circumstances and in the interest of removing doubt about the fairness of a given decision. The number of grievances can serve as a barometer of the organizational climate (i.e., staff relations) of an agency.

The litigation of grievances is time-consuming and costly for unions. Resolving disputes by binding arbitration is not without its benefits. It serves to reassure employees that the union is backing them in disputes with management. The union reaps the benefit of the publicity and "brownie points" generated by arbitration proceedings.

Aside from salaries and fringe benefits, the grievance procedure is clearly the union's strongest selling point. A formal grievance procedure also protects the union from work stoppages, altercations, and sabotage. In other words, it spares the union from having to organize wildcat strikes and job actions while informing management about the state of morale, supervisory practices, and workers' needs.

Training. Training in municipal personnel systems may be defined as the formal and informal skill development required for job-related tasks. Training ranges from foremen or supervisors orienting workers in the use of new techniques or new machinery to attendance at university courses taught at the request of city agencies. Preservice training involves teaching the job skills required of individuals within a particular job description. Police and firemen, for example, receive elaborate preservice training in classrooms and also spend some time in apprenticeships. Other employees are often required to have certain training before assignment (e.g., clerical and computer training). Still others are only required to possess a high school diploma or to have fulfilled the requirements for a college degree. A few positions (e.g., those of physician, lawyer, or accountant) require that the employee belong to certain accredited professional organizations.

After assignment to a department, an employee may be given in-service training. In-service training includes skill updating, retraining, sensitivity training (i.e., human relations), and career development. In-service training may also be occasioned by the advent of new technology (e.g., word-processing equipment), changes in regulations (i.e., changes in federal, state, and local statutes), and general-skill obsolescence. The greatest part of skill training is carried out by supervisors, who regard such training as part of their job description. Supervisors rarely seek outside assistance in educating their subordinates. Self-development training, or continuing education, is initiated by employees seeking more credentials, promotion, or visibility.

Since the 1975 charter revision, career development and skill updating have become primarily the responsibility of the agency personnel department or division. In the relationship between the city's Department of Personnel and the agency training staff, two norms prevail: the norm of nonintervention and the norm of extra resources. The norm of nonintervention states that training programs and evaluations must be initiated by the line agency. The central personnel office does not impose training requirements on agencies, but makes itself available as a resource. Any joint training program is a matter of negotiation between the line supervisor, personnel division, and central office.

The norm of extra resources states that a manager's enthusiasm for training is conditioned by who is paying for the training. If the training is funded by federal, state, or foundation monies, it is good. If it comes out of the operating budget, the money could be better spent. Line managers often resent having workers attend training sessions because such attendance means that the managers will be shorthanded because of worker absence. Therefore, employees are not motivated to take training courses inasmuch as these will not enhance either promotion opportunities or salary increments. Promotions are determined by examinations, available openings, and internal office politics. Salaries are often determined by union contracts.

The lack of incentive for training encourages obsolescence and insularity among employees. Moreover, it is common to find high-ranking agency professionals whose reading habits include only department memos and regulations. Many do not read books and journal articles about their profession nor attend professional conferences. A few have developed antitraining biases that make it difficult for management to promote such programs. For this reason, training has become an orphan with no one willing to claim it as a legitimate part of the organizational family.

Training as Patronage. One of the important functions of external training is patronage utility. Because training has become a multimillion-dollar business, many profit and nonprofit agencies have obtained contracts to train city employees. Only agencies with good political connections can hope to get city contracts. The vendors court city officials and encourage them to use more training manuals and equipment, and they, in turn, lobby for more in-service training for public employees.

The written contract with a fancy management or training agency is rarely detected as patronage. Developing training manuals and conducting seminars for city agencies seem to be a lucrative and growing enterprise. Many former city officials work in these agencies or sit on their boards of directors.

THE NORM OF NEGOTIATION AND SPONSORSHIP

As noted before, personnel policy is not made in a vacuum, nor is it politically benign. Each rule change brings a corresponding shift in power among participants. The instability of the system protects it from fossilization. The problems of the Personnel Department can be traced to its evolution during the twentieth-century periods of reform. The academic reformers underestimated the political environment of their standard bearer (the personnel director) and never anticipated the possibility of a civil servant ascending to that post. The personnel director was never given adequate tools to defend himself against encroachment from the budget director. Thus the office became an easy target for frustrated agency heads, and the charter revision of 1975 was in part a result of that frustration.

Fortunately the new reformers—the fiscal managers—did not seek to strengthen the powers of the personnel director as they sought solutions to the fiscal crisis. Preoccupied as they have been with budget balancing and fiscal images, they may arrive at a new yet classic dichotomy: manpower versus budget. In any case, if they want to achieve their goal of a balanced budget, they must conform to the norm of negotiation.

The norm of negotiation mandates that all policy issues be negotiable. The way to solve problems is to agree on common goals and then isolate and negotiate differences. The norm of negotiation means that there is no zero-sum game. Everyone gains something, and there are no losers in absolute terms. The new fiscal managers must be willing to make

accommodations if they hope to participate effectively in the city's political processes.

The norm of negotiation applies to the Schrag case as well as to the sponsorship of bureau chiefs and managers. These two examples suggest that human dimensions are critical factors in the personnel recruitment process. Formal procedures and examinations do not offset the impact of informal groupings. People resort to social selections and cliques to protect themselves from insiders, outsiders, and critics. In other words, bureaucrats are the same as the rest of humanity in believing that "the best person for the role are my friends and me."

SUMMARY

From a technical standpoint, as we have already stated, the New York City personnel administration structure hardly employs the principles lauded in public-management textbooks. There are tens, perhaps hundreds, of persons with either veto or delaying power in the employee-relations area. This being the case, any disgruntled and resourceful individual can slow down the wheels of a multimillion-dollar operation. One civil servant interviewed described the situation as very democratic. Yet another considered personnel procedures chaotic, confusing, and counterproductive.

It is clear that with the city's attempt to have multiple-access points and -review mechanisms within its structure, it has saddled itself with top-heavy personnel machinery. In return, the city receives little visible benefit, and the situation is extremely costly. Participants in the system do not see it as the optimum way to conduct employee relations but rather as the preferred way. They like the confusion, the overlapping and duplicative agencies, the vague regulations, the outside appeals system of the courts and local politicians, and the sheer drama of working in one of the most fascinating soap operas in urban America today.

An examination of the structure's nuts and bolts tells us something about the design of the classification, promotion, and compensation systems. These are the personnel areas of politics. Among the factors that facilitate working relationships are the social friendships among the key actors involved in the drama by means of which everyone claims to be an intimate social friend of his or her political rival. These acknowledgments of friendship seem genuine, but the real function of such social meetings is to provide a mechanism for bypassing the various barriers in employee relationships.

7

SUMMARY AND RECOMMENDATIONS

The central purpose of this book has been to assess the impact of interest-group interaction on public-employment policies in New York City. The personnel policy-making process has been determined by interacting groups that have competed for power through the allocation of resources and status. This struggle has been examined in the light of the conflict between Tammany and the genteel reformers (1824–1898), the coexistence of Tammany and the genteel reformers (1898–1914), the conflict between Tammany and the academic reformers (1914–1916), the coexistence of Tammany and the academic reformers (1916–1954), and the conflict between the academic reformers and the unions (1954 to the present). Other participants have intermittently joined in these conflicts, including the press (e.g., Thomas Nast's cartoons of Tammany), management consultants (e.g., David Stanley's manpower study), and the state legislature (e.g., the so-called Lyons' residency law).

The general public also plays a role in personnel policy making. Its members are asked to participate, contribute, and support the interest group of their choice. After identifying their potential allies, interest groups have been able to enlist certain segments of the public's support in the struggle for control of municipal personnel. For example, the genteel reformers were able to persuade religious leaders to endorse their campaign for a more meritorious personnel system; unions were able to kindle support in the poor communities by championing affirmative action and the expansion of welfare services.

Interaction among contending personnel groups does not necessarily lead toward equilibrium. By distinguishing between the regular and intermittent participants, the thesis of this book is that no one group makes personnel policy single-handedly. This is not to gainsay the fact that some groups have access to a great number of resources, enjoy a certain visibility, have attentive audiences, and can dominate the scene at almost any given moment. But the domination is fleeting and is usually accompanied by a number of limitations. For example, despite the enormous political strength of the unions, labor organizations are powerless to improve productivity among workers, to bolster morale, or to insure absolute compliance with the rules of the workplace.

Conscription, normative persuasion, and coercion have been the primary methods used for recruiting group members. For example, unions with the help of politicians and the courts have been able to establish agency shops in city government (i.e., nonunion members must pay a service fee to unions instead of dues). Union dues and fees are collected automatically by withdrawing the amount from workers' paychecks. Academic reformers have been able to recruit their university colleagues by advocating more education among public employees. University officials have expanded their curricula and accepted contracts for the training and research of the city personnel system. Fiscal managers, themselves drafted by the investment community, tried to reorient the city accounts and bookkeeping methods. The new accounting procedure of the 1975 charter revision has facilitated the recruitment of fiscal bureaucrats.

Participation in the city's Personnel Department is not without its separate and selective benefits. These may be in the form of income or in the opportunity to participate in personnel decisions, patronage, and public recognition. Benefits are only allocated to official members of a particular group. Union members receive higher wages and a pension, are in on the latest union news, and receive various health and education benefits. Reformers, who have a political reputation for being "fighters," cash in on their reputation when they run for public office (e.g., LaGuardia). Citizens Union and the City Club have both enjoyed having considerable influence in the personnel arena. They have been able to legitimate most of their demands for change as drives for reform.

Throughout this book an attempt has been made to alert the reader to the drama of group politics and to provide a frame of reference for evaluating the postures and roles of the actors on the political scene. Municipal personnel politics represents, however, far more than entertainment; it is a deadly serious struggle for power and influence. In other words, the competition for jobs and income—namely, the opportunity to work—is analogous to a game of musical chairs—without enough chairs to go around. Each group, consciously or unconsciously, tries to leave the competing groups standing without a chair. To top it all off, the winners are never satisfied with winning, but find it necessary to justify their prize. They use the theater of politics to defend their claims to public jobs and income.

Every group adopts a rhetorical style and a special strategy aimed at rallying its constituency and persuading the general public. The personnel arena constitutes not merely a divergence of interests, but also a divergence of political style. Ascendent groups speak out boldly for the future; threatened groups search for ways to lay blame and to seek redemption. The former style is generally open, positive, and resolute; the latter confused, vindictive, and uncertain. Each group is a defender of a particular set of values and interests. Its political style and behavior changes in response to real or imagined challenges from other groups.

New York City politics has always been characterized by a colorful theatrical tradition. It has produced people like Everett Wheeler, Edwin Godkin, Boss Tweed, Robert Moses, Fiorello LaGuardia. The city can boast of a great and enduring tradition of liberal reform that has added a certain *pièce bien faite*—a unique flavor—to its politics. Interest-group politics provides its own melodrama. Group players mask themselves as tribunes of the working class and as defenders of humanitarian and civil-libertarian principles. Players recite scripts and practice their craft on unsuspecting individuals. Just like Shakespeare's drunken porter in *Macbeth,* ad hoc advocate groups and grass-roots leaders that champion the causes of the unrepresented class (e.g., Citizens Against Westway) furnish relief from the intensity of the main plot. Such histrionics make for great theater, all the while providing a reliable strategy for group achievement.

The members of the political opposition, viz., the fiscal conservatives, have been unable—to use a present-day colloquialism—to get their act together. Their rhetoric seems more appropriate to the nineteenth century than prescriptive for the future. Conservatives have allowed themselves to be cast in the roles of prigs, naysayers, and obstructionists. But their biggest problem is that they have lost the flair for eloquence. Lacking the exhilarating rhetoric of their opponents, they have found no way to develop the audience needed to support their positions. The dull and old-fashioned theater of the conservatives lacks maneuverability in the municipal personnel arena.

Reformers and Personnel Policy. Reading New York City's civil service history is analogous to being involved in a melodrama. It is full of adventure (e.g., the antics of Tammany bosses, fighting reformers, and journalists), suspense (the unpredictable rhetoric of Mayor Gaynor), and romance (the personal life of the flamboyant Jimmy Walker).

Many observers of New York City politics prefer to believe that the regular party politicians and bureaucrats are the bad guys and the reformers are the good ones, except that in this script the good guys are always fighting a hopeless battle with the bad. The conventional wisdom is that the good folks are occasionally able to score small victories, but once the pressure and publicity have ended, the bad apples return to politics as usual.

This theme is reflected in the myth of the reform cycle in New York City politics.[1] The fact is that the reformers have been incredibly successful in imposing their views and values on city politics. They have never been antiestablishment outsiders but a part of the drama that facilitates political change. Neither have they been altruists. In fact, their political activities might be characterized as self-serving. Contemporary reformers are unquestionably seeking to expand middle-class job opportunities in municipal government. Once reformers are seen in these terms, then the surrealistic quality of New York City politics becomes understandable.

In Chapter 2, the theater of good guys (or reformers) was presented. These actors promised to cleanse the body politic and save the city from the perils of spoilsmen. They read their parts well but were unconvincing. The good guys, however, provided the spectacles: Colonel Waring's White Wings (sanitationmen) sweeping the city streets in white uniforms; John Purroy Mitchel's preaching the gospel of efficiency; and LaGuardia's razzle-dazzle and his comic-page reading during a newspaper strike. Journalists and the public remember these administrations as the golden era of city politics because of the flamboyant political styles and sideshows, or what Ferdinand Mount has called the "road shows of politicians."

Politicians who walk among the people or engage in symbolic gestures can later mask an otherwise lackluster performance. The public expects and wants clichés, apothegms, and oxymora rather than carefully stated arguments on policy. Murray Edelman has made a similar observation:

It is characteristic of large numbers of people in our society that they see and think in terms of stereotypes, personalization and oversimplifications, that they cannot recognize or tolerate ambiguous and complex situations, and that they accordingly respond chiefly to symbols that oversimplify and distort. This form of behavior (together with other characteristics less relevant to the political process) is especially likely to occur where there is insecurity occasioned by failure to adjust to real or perceived problems.[2]

So it is with the audience for New York City politics. The people enjoy a good show. Few remember the important administrative changes (e.g., Lindsay's reorganization plan) and charter-revision fights. They recall Mike Quill, leader of the Transit Workers' union and the transit strike; former Miss America Bess Meyerson and the consumer crusade; and the Con Edison blackouts. Is this the informed public that political theorists believe is essential to a democracy? One could argue that the average individual has a limited attention span and a modest capacity for political analysis. Many people prefer to be satisfied with rather than knowledgeable about public affairs. Believing that they lack the time and energy to achieve political competence, most people are generally willing to acquiesce to the judgment of their political leaders; they also may resent politicians who solicit suggestions from the public or admit that there are no simple solutions to problems. Most political actors, on the other hand, are not rationalist—at least, not in their rhetoric.

Some leaders see themselves as the vanguard for change and as pathfinders promoting the validity of their causes. Each in their own way gets caught up in the drama of events. The critical question is, Is it possible for the audience to confuse these histrionics with the substantive political issues before the city? The current review of the personnel scene suggests, as has Ferdinand Mount, that it is impossible to separate the two. Given the size of the city of New York, neither can be safely ignored in the governing process, a point Mount has made with some skill:

We have argued that in large, complex, modern societies which can function only by representative government the dialogue is under particular strain. The sense of distance lends awkwardness to the expression of familiar sentiments and everyday requests. The political actor's task is to diminish this sense of distance, to shorten the lines of communication, both literally by talking directly to as many of his constituents as he can, and figuratively by creating a sense of intimacy.... The political actor is both interpreter and protagonist, both observer and participant. He has a duty to the public and a duty to his own conscience, mirroring the antinomy between sociological fact and values. There is further duality in his roles: the disproportion between the banal business of politics—the conciliation of interests and passions, the bargaining and brokering—and the precious hopes and fears, the elevated morale and spiritual principles which are at stake.[3]

This disproportion helps the political audience to accept the major shifts in the economic structure of the city and the endless contradictions in the content of public policy. It seems clear that there has always been a linkage between changes in economic conditions and uses of public-sector jobs. As New York City shifted from a shipping-mercantile economy to industrial capitalism and finally to financial capitalism, the city's services expanded to meet the needs of the new types of workers. The supply of manpower quickly outgrew job opportunities.

The immigrants who came to New York looking for work brought ambition and social problems with them. Social-service work, once the domain of private charities, was politicized by Tammany Hall. As the population grew, the city government assumed the major responsibility for social services, relief activities became more formalized and professionalized. A new professional class termed social workers became a permanent part of the city's bureaucracy. When the manufacturing industries began to abandon the city, the unemployed needed more, not fewer, social services. The city developed an array of social-service programs that often rivaled those of the federal government (e.g., the Department of Health, Education and Welfare). The new public-sector economy was able to accommodate most of the excess of professional service workers. But this expansion of the economy meant a new reliance on a large and permanent class of unemployed and unemployable workers. Any economy that depends on the largess of federal social-service resources and the misfortunes of the poor is a risky one indeed.

As the economy changed, so did the histrionics. The major difference in the political theater was not in substance but in style, caused by the demands of the electronic media. This new form of communication required better players (i.e., politicians and union leaders) before the cameras and microphones, and more capable technicians behind the scenes (i.e., public employees). The prospect for improvements in the performance of these players is guarded, for the interest groups in the personnel arena remain committed to the politicization of recruitment.

Civil Service Recruitment and the Open Bureaucracy. The city bureaucracy provided a route to middle-class membership, a first step in a working career, a source of petty and grand patronage, a forum for minority-group aspiration, a source of ethnic identity and cohesion, a theater of sentiment and absurdity, a revenue conduit, and a general scapegoat for any real or imagined ills in urban living. New York City has been able to be all these diverse things because it accepted the ethics of vertical recruitment. The principle of selecting department leaders from within has also prevented anything analogous to the ancient Chinese caste of mandarins or the "closing tendency."

New York City civil servants are not now nor have they ever been a caste of mandarins—i.e., a civil service aristocracy. The antimandarinist tradition in the city's work force has been maintained primarily by third-party intervention. Interest groups have inserted themselves between the elected official and the bureaucracy. The early interventions were made by the political machine, and more recently by the reformers. In civil service history, both the genteel and academic reformers worked to increase the mayor's administrative control over the selection of city workers. The bureaucracy has never been autonomous, nor has it been free of blatant examples of patronage. In other words, the city has many problems, but mandarinism is not one of them.

The open bureaucracy has to be considered a truly American invention. Our society's choice of a decentralized representative democracy precludes an absolutely efficient bureaucracy. Episodic mismanagement is the price of democracy. The occasional demonstration of massive inefficiency confirms that the system has not succumbed to the "closing tendency," or the propensity of bureaucrats to deny public access to the internal management of an agency. This exclusionary, self-righteous, self-serving and nefarious attitude has been a common problem among educated civil servants.

Max Weber, the famous German sociologist, has argued:

Democracy must oppose bureaucracy as a tendency towards a caste of mandarins, removed from the common people by expert training, examination certificates, and tenure of office, but the scope of administrative functions, the end of the open frontier, and the narrowing of opportunities make the spoils system, with its public waste, irregularities, and lack of technical efficiency increasingly impossible and undemocratic. Thus, democracy has to promote what reason demands and democratic sentiment hates.[4]

Parties and Personnel Policy. As E. E. Schattschneider suggested long ago, political parties are the keystones of our democracy.[5] Without them we cannot have representative or accountable bureaucracies. Civil service reformers in their zeal to rid the cities of petty patronage managed to displace the political parties in the personnel recruitment process. The parties now function at the margin of the personnel system and are effective only in grand patronage. (For this reason, consequently, parties have become useful only to the middle class. The political clubs of New York are loose social groups organized to serve the interest of a single local officeholder or middle-class job seeker.) The demise of party influence in personnel policy has left the bureaucracy poorer and opened a serious flaw in our participatory democracy.

United States Supreme Court Justice Powell recognized this factor in his dissent in *Elrod* v. *Burns*. He argued cogently that patronage stimulates public interest in local affairs, serves as a vehicle for information, and generates funding for local organizations. He furthermore observed:

Patronage hiring practices also enable party organizations to persist and function at the local level. Such organizations become visible to the electorate at large only at election time, but the dull periods between elections require ongoing activities: precinct organizations must be maintained; new voters registered; and minor political "chores" performed for citizens who otherwise may have no practical means of access to officeholders. In some communities, party organizations and clubs also render helpful social services.

It is naive to think that these types of political activities are motivated at these levels by some academic interest in "democracy" or other public service impulse.[6]

Courts, State Legislators, and Personnel Policy. Justice Powell's position on local patronage is among his profession unique. Most jurists manage to find constitutional issues lurking in local personnel practices, conflicts, and controversies. As a result, some lawyers are eager to test municipal civil service rules in the federal courts. Judicial review has produced a disruptive and cooling effect on civil service regulations. Personnel directors now consult lawyers in order to write administrative procedures. Federal courts inveigh against discriminatory practices. State courts strike down municipal residency codes. Local courts play a major role in labor negotiations and civil service rule disputes. All this litigation has added to the cost of maintaining a civil service system and to the confusion that now characterizes the rights of employees and the obligations of management.

Since the inception of municipal civil service reform, the state legislature has maintained an active interest in New York City personnel policy. The state government has investigated corruption in city departments, created charter-revision commissions, and enacted overlapping and redundant employment laws. As the ultimate authority in civil service matters, the state legislature has allowed itself to be courted by municipal-personnel interest groups. These groups have discovered that any policy decisions made by local officials can be appealed to the state legislatures. The propensity to intervene in the city's personnel policy began in the early Tammany Hall years. The upstate Republican machine used the state legislature for leverage in disputes with Tammany. Today the complex financial relationship between the city and the state provide new grounds for continued legislative intervention in city affairs. The presence of the state legislature in municipal personnel affairs has further fragmented personnel policy making in New York City.

The Mayor and Personnel Policy. New York City mayors have varied greatly in terms of interest, skills, ideology, and opportunity with regard to municipal personnel policy. Some mayors have seen this policy as the touchstone of efficient government (e.g., William Strong and John P. Mitchel). Others have tended to ignore the personnel system (Vincent Impellitteri). Still others have sought major changes in existing policies (Fiorello LaGuardia and Robert Wagner). A few have allowed the reform policies of predecessors to wither away for lack of support (e.g., Robert Van Wick). Only one mayor thought that civil servants were the best judges of personnel policies (Abraham Beame).

At present the mayor tends to support the academic reformers' notion of a personnel director free of any civil service commission's legislative review. Reformers have apparently convinced mayors that personnel directors are more amenable to mayoral directives. History suggests, however, that a personnel director with strong mayoral support is no match for entrenched interest groups. Even in those rare occasions when a mayor enjoys all of Professor Pressman's preconditions for leadership— fiscal resources, staff resources, policy jurisdiction, media access, party support, and an adequate salary—he or she cannot make policy alone; he or she must always seek alliances with other interest groups. As we have suggested in this book, the various interest groups are more con-cerned with maintaining the status quo than promoting the career or preference of any particular mayor. It is because of this situation that most mayors, if prudent, resort to symbolic interaction in order to salvage at least the reputation of being an effective superintendent of the city's personnel policies.

Unions and Personnel Policy. The ability of the unions to create drama makes them a powerful interest group indeed. They can bring attention to themselves by threatening strikes and work slowdowns, and by inflam-matory speeches. Their swashbuckling leaders are a part of the frontier fantasy of most New York City dwellers. The public seems always to enjoy listening to their criticisms of the mayor. Union leaders are among city residents who became media stars in the seventies. Because they were interesting and powerful men, they were deemed newsworthy, and they could command the attention and imagination of the public.

Unions and collective bargaining have resulted in making public service more competitive within the private sector by providing better salaries and benefits to workers. The unions, strong supporters of the merit system and vertical recruitment, have also shared in the selection of department commissioners and their aides. By negotiating matters of promotion and organizational work rules, they have consolidated their alliances with informal worker groups. Union support of vertical recruitment has brought more reliance on test scores for promotion, as well as resistance to lateral-entrance schemes which involve restricting the mobility of its members.

By stressing economic security, the unions have raised the stakes of their membership's "side bets"—namely, investments in salaries and benefits—thereby further locking union members into their departments. The increase in side bets has not, however, alleviated the problem of estrangement or status deprivation among workers. The morale problem has been largely ignored by the union leaders, who are forced to engage in the politics of compensation in order to stay in office.

The intervention of unions in the rule-making process has been most unfortunate because it has eroded the authority of civil service managers. The relative powerlessness of civil service managers vis-à-vis the unions may account for the sense of alienation and status deprivation found in this study. Union leaders often complain about the low quality of management in the city without admitting that they are partially responsible for it.

Despite their success, the unions are still a threatened group. They have invested financially so heavily in the city that they must assume a more politically conservative fiscal position in the future. To avoid losing their gains and their leaders' reputations as swashbucklers, they have to depend more and more on the media for support and publicity. Michael Lipsky has found ominous implications for that kind of dependence:

To the extent that successful protest activity depends on appealing to and/or threatening other groups in the community, the communications media set the limits of protest action. If protest tactics are not considered significant by the media, or if newspaper and television reporters or editors decide to overlook protest tactics, protest organization will not succeed. Like the tree falling unheard in the forest there is no protest unless it is perceived and projected.[7]

In any case, union leaders have found themselves increasingly on the defensive. Although there have been lately few counterbalancing groups, new ones will surely emerge with different messages, claims, and mobilizing techniques. It will be interesting to see how the unions react to their replacement by the fiscal managers now on the stage of New York City politics. Adjusting to a declining group status may be the most difficult role for these men of action to play.

Personnel Policy and Structural-Procedural Reform. The evidence seems to suggest that prescriptive and structural inventions (e.g., the lay Civil Service Commission and personnel directorship) failed to achieve parity with other departments in the city government. The legitimacy and the activities of these offices have been successfully challenged by both friend and foe. The evidence also suggests that procedural reforms—e.g., position-classification schemes, job audits, and regulations—have not offset the politics of personnel policies. Unable to avoid the bane of entangling alliances, shifting coalitions, and patronage vendors, New York City's struggle to maintain a credible management posture continues.

Professionalism has yet to become part of the ethos of the city bureaucracy. Most civil servants want to preserve their job routines and privileges rather than respond to opportunities for job challenges. In other words, prescriptive reforms have not achieved the intended results, but have only served to promote more interest-group politics (e.g., the written examination created a market for professional test takers, preparatory manual publishers, and technical schools). Consequently, personnel policy has continued to change, but the goal of efficient government remains elusive.

One lasting impression gained from the interviews conducted with civil servants and personnel officials in New York City in conjunction with the present study was the virtually total lack of any belief in the efficacy of management as a social science. The men and women who managed the city departments cared little about the wonders of operations research, economic modeling, and survey analysis. They sought only to cope with a demanding public, wayward subordinates, and a highly politicized environment. Academics who think otherwise should ponder the words of a city manager:

PPBS, MBO, ZBB, and all those alphabet-soup things are just fads. They come and go. They are a nuisance. You have to learn them, and then some other guy invents another toy. Then you start again. It is like being on a treadmill. You don't get anywhere, but you burn up a lot of energy. I have had fancy management courses. Believe me, it doesn't work in this department. . . . Besides people know when you are trying to put them out of a job. The unions would eat me alive if I tried to implement that management stuff.[8]

The last sentence in this statement reminds us that unions are considerably more of an immediate problem and threat for municipal personnel managers than technology is. Labor organizations have imbued city personnel politics with excitement, fear, and rancor.

Recommendations. When Wallace Sayre and Herbert Kaufman wrote their 1960 classic, *Governing New York City,* the United States was enjoying a period of élan where almost anything seemed possible. In 1973 the New York City government, with 380,000 permanent and part-time employees and a budget of $14 billion, seemed unshakable. Unfortunately, the economic foundation of the system collapsed, and the city found itself on the long road toward retrenchment. Today we live in a period of resignation and lowered expectations, and the city seems to be in an irreversible decline.

The 1975 fiscal crisis revived the notion that someone behind the scenes was manipulating city politics. Even those erstwhile insightful journalists Newfield and DuBrul were seduced by the idea of what they called a "permanent government." Although they included many interest groups in their permanent government, there is still no empirical evidence to prove that the leaders of those interest groups who came to the city's aid in its hour of peril are the real power wielders in the political arena. Sayre and Kaufman's comment still holds true for New York City politics:

The most lasting impressions created by a systematic analysis of New York City's political and governmental system as a whole are of its democratic virtues: its qualities of openness, its commitments to bargaining and accommodation among participants, its receptivity to new participants, its opportunities for the exercise of leadership, and unmatched variety and number of the city's residents new and old.[9]

It may be added that the theater of city politics is too ephemeral for cabals. Often the best-rehearsed performances are flops (e.g., the first appearance of academic reformers in the Mitchel administration). Success in the public personnel arena seems to be a combination of timing, audience appeal, and economic circumstances. Even the traditional political bargaining and negotiation among interest groups have become a part of the public spectacle. Sunshine laws and television cameras in legislative chambers are evidence that the public wants to see and hear more about this facet of the policy-making process.

From this review of New York City's personnel politics, it would appear that any prognosis for nontheatrical or rational management systems must be guarded. The city's work force will probably always be too large, too costly, too inefficient. It can neither be replaced nor effectively reformed. Unfortunately, this is a lesson that each governing interest group has to learn for itself. Leaders of ascendent groups rarely listen to the political admonitions of descendent ones. Groups will in every likelihood continue to reinvent the Wilsonian model (separating politics from administration), to rehabilitate Taylorism, and to profess faith in technology; and the public will accept these myths as long as they are well packaged and presented.

The failure of the 1979 civil service reform package was a serious blow to the Koch administration and to the mayor's effort to return the mayoralty to the center of the personnel management stage. This was largely so because it demonstrated that Koch and his staff had not done their political homework (i.e., counting votes and negotiating a compromise before the formal presentation of the package). The defeat also showed that the mayor had neglected to consult either thoroughly or properly members of the personnel community.

The ad hoc Taxpayers Campaign for Civil Service Reform, chaired by Howard Samuels, which included within its ranks a number of prominent politicians and organizations, was an inappropriate mechanism for change. Aside from being a newcomer to the municipal personnel community, Samuels was not an official member of any of the relevant interest groups. What was to have been a taxpayers' campaign turned out to be a noncampaign, relying on press releases and organizational endorsements for its impact. The stakes in the personnel conflict were simply too high for such an ad hoc campaign to enjoy any success.

Aside from political miscalculations, the Koch administration has also made some dubious assumptions about the personnel community. The proposals that attempt to prohibit supervisors and subordinates from belonging to the same union assume that ending an obvious conflict of interest will insure the loyalty of the managers. This may very well not be. A manager's organizational loyalty presently seems to be far more connected with side bets—matters of pension, tenure, and status. Young workers no longer are loyal to the extant administration, because there are job opportunities to be had at another level of government or in the private sector. For this reason, the city administration should concentrate on building a career development plan that will retain young managers. The municipal administration can make more lower level managerial jobs more interesting and satisfying.

The Koch proposal (i.e., prohibiting common union membership for managers and workers) will also encounter opposition from managers themselves. The unions are the largest and most effective workers advocate group in the personnel community. They have achieved unparalleled wage increases and benefits and can veto any management rule. Few professional organizations (e.g., the Managerial Employee Association) can match their political power. It is therefore in the financial and political interest of a manager to be in a union with subordinates.

Moreover, the separation of managers and subordinates would create more bargaining units, which is a direct contradiction of another Koch proposal to consolidate bargaining units.

The proposals by Mayor Koch would also allow the appointment of temporary managerial personnel—three year tenures—that would be at variance with the merit principle and thus against vertical mobility. A possible two-track system of organizational upward mobility might develop, also affecting the morale of the workplace. Those people who were on a three-year tenure would have positional authority but lack technical authority. This might well cause problems with organizational compliance. Bureaucrats may not necessarily listen to managers who do not spring from among the ranks. This provision would also wipe out the mentor-sponsor system that weeds out unobligated entrepreneurs. Workers in the mentor-sponsor system have attempted to socialize managerial candidates to organizational needs, mitigating the possibility of empire building and show boating.

The provision to expand the exempt classes—e.g., political appointees—has been a traditional tactic of reformers and partisans. Reformers started to expand the exempt classes under Mayor Strong, and they continued under Mayor LaGuardia. Mayor Koch's desire to extend the exempt classes is therefore in the reform tradition.

The Koch reform package proposed a one-in-ten rule that would give all recruiters more discretion in selecting candidates for employment. To reform the selection process is difficult for the reasons cited in this book. A better strategy might be to change the recruiters. The city might use recruitment teams that include civilians. If the city decided to retain the present recruitment process, there might be a more comprehensive and integrated set of guidelines defining the requisites of prospective applicants. Citizens Union makes this point in its critique of Mayor Koch's management plan.

The proposal for the transfer of public employees without their consent would give the administration more flexibility and would reduce the insularity of the managerial class. While generally a welcome change, involuntary transfer might in certain cases be seen as punishment should supervisors be inclined only to transfer "bad apples." (Union leaders would prefer transfers to be negotiated rather than leave their membership open to other administrators.)

A transfer policy might be possible and justifiable during a time of fiscal crisis, but any worker would soon expect his or her union to reinstitute a policy that made the location of the workplace consistent with seniority. Then the problem of employee's seniority rights presents itself. The proposal to assign equal weight to seniority and performance evaluations sounds like an old academic reform idea. Unfortunately, it is quite difficult to define acceptable measures of performance. Moreover, there is a heavy burden on the evaluator. As one civil servant asserted, "Performance is in the eye of the beholder."

Should performance become crucial in a worker's career, there may be an increase in litigation over performance evaluation. Supervisors will be reluctant to give poor ratings except in extreme cases. There will also be the problem of distinguishing between personality conflicts and poor performance. One can easily envision a lawsuit that alleges personality conflict as the cause of a poor evaluation. In such cases, careers may be injured and entangled in legal adjudication.

Given these conditions, it seems that proposals for more civil-service reforms are illusory and futile. One cannot, however, argue that we have reached the end of policy originality in city politics. A conceptual breakthrough is possible, but any strategy must keep the following few thoughts in mind:

1. The personnel arena is full of veto groups that can operate in unison or separately.

2. Any reduction in city services and personnel will affect the working poor first and foremost. It may seriously delay their opportunity to use city jobs to lift themselves or their children out of poverty.

3. The federal government is not an honest broker in city politics, as the city continues to rely on Congress for help with its budget.

4. Fiscal home rule is no longer a means for evaluating a city that performs a critical national function.

5. Charter revision no longer represents an effective way to redistribute political power. The new fiscal managers weren't granted power; they seized it. Neither can Charter revision institutionalize these managers in the government. Hegemony has to be earned and maintained. In other words, the new fiscal managers will have to become gladiators or be replaced by rival interest groups.

6. The answer to the fiscal crisis is not more money but more jobs. Unless and until there is a strong private sector economy, the city faces the prospect of a permanent budget deficit.

There is no magic formula leading to change in existing conditions in the city's municipal personnel employment. Meaningful change requires new ideas, new myths, and new people. Municipal workers can survive an occasional episode of mismanagement, but the city's infrastructure will decay if the interest groups do not agree on a new set of fiscal rules.

Implications for Other Cities. If one were to generalize about municipal personnel politics from the single example of New York City to all other cities, a grave injustice would be done to those with different histories and different political environments. Many of the elements that make up the New York City system may be because of the city's size. Smaller cities might never experience the personnel and fiscal problems of New York. Yet the generalizations are applicable in studying the possible future urban personnel policies of growing cities.

There are a number of things to be learned from the personnel drama in New York. First, if a city decides to depend heavily on performance appraisals for rehiring, layoff, and salary decisions, public officials should be aware of the limitations of written appraisals. Aside from the problems of constructing an objective rating scale, selecting and training the evaluators will require a considerable amount of time and resources. Unions will attempt to negotiate the entire appraisal process, including the weight of written appraisals or promotions, and workers will attempt to routinize the evaluation process.

Workers can put pressure on supervisors either by threatening job actions, appeals to the personnel department, or by filing grievance forms. If subordinates personalize the process, the real value of the appraisal is lost. Reliance on these appraisals at the expense of workbench sociology (i.e., its effect on staff morale and supervisor-subordinate relations) can cause line or operating agency problems. In other words, objective personnel assessments are not amenable to highly politicized environments.

Subordinates should be active participants in the performance appraisal process. Otherwise, as Professor Douglas McGregor concluded:

It places the manager in the untenable position of judging the personal worth of his subordinates, and of acting on these judgments. No manager possesses nor should he acquire the skill necessary to carry out this responsibility effectively. Few would be even willing to accept it if they were fully aware of the implications.[10]

McGregor's admonition is even more true today since interest groups dominate the policy process and the courts are entertaining more cases in personnel rights. As mentioned earlier, legal problems dissuade managers from accepting this responsibility. Therefore, it is suggested that city governments incorporate performance appraisals in their inservice training programs for managers and workers.

Second, productivity should be negotiated at the workbench and not at the contract table. The experience in New York City suggests that unions do not have any control over member productivity. Although union leadership has proven quite skilled at the negotiation of productivity goals and in linking these goals to cost-of-living allowances, the leader cannot deliver. During the New York City financial crisis, fiscal managers were lured into contract agreements which specified productivity goals. These goals were never met. The *New York Times* reported this outcome, published in a small column practically hidden within the newspaper,[11] but the public apparently forgot the issue altogether (a reaction predicted by the labor leaders interviewed for this study). City departments resorted to organizational and time gimmicks (i.e., reducing the rest period, eliminating coffee breaks, and reassigning clerical help) to meet their goals.

If a city is serious about raising the productivity level of the public sector, it should bypass the unions. Workers should be allowed to share in goal-setting directly and should be given group, rather than individual, credit. The practice of awarding a thousand dollars, for example, to one individual for accomplishment serves as a disincentive for group productivity. Prize winners are often not the role models for an agency. A more effective strategy would be a team approach (e.g., recognition at the precinct, district, or neighborhood level). This would create competition and instill group pride in the team's accomplishments. Under this plan, public recognition and other group incentives might induce greater productivity and worker creativity.

Third, public employee unions should resist the advice of the legal profession and should not attempt to codify all employee relationships into law. Understandably, public labor lawyers seek to increase their influence in the personnel community by converting political issues into legal ones. The increase of personnel law is the epitome of proceduralism and bureaucratization. Unions have spent enormous sums of money hiring others to do what they should be able to accomplish by sitting down at the contract table. Unions should return to the substantive issues, such as designing ways of providing cost-efficient services and promoting job-enriching experiences for their members. Otherwise, worker alienation may threaten the entire personnel community. As this research has suggested, wage increases alone cannot increase morale.

Fourth, in motivation and in education, workers in the public sphere are equal to those in private corporations. Because there are no profit margins or units of production, however, the public employee cannot be compared directly with his or her private counterpart. Moreover, the quality of work for both groups seems to be about the same. Unfortunately, the public employee is still considered a second-rate worker by the general citizenry. Municipal government, therefore, could help to improve the image of its workers by educating the public at large. (In New York, for instance, the American Federation of State, County, and Municipal Employees—AFSCME of the AFL–CIO—has produced a television commercial which shows city workers smiling and giving the appearance of caring about people. This is a step in the right direction.)

Finally, it is necessary to return to the idea of reforming work practices rather than the civil service. After reviewing the history of some years of municipal civil service reform, one is struck by the futility of procedural reform and chagrined by the politicization of the personnel community. Urban personnel policy is between Scylla and Charybdis—in other words, between two equally hazardous alternatives. Cities cannot safely ignore procedural reform and thereby risk losing complete control of city management, nor can they allow politics to dictate their entire personnel and administrative policies. Therefore, more reliance upon the employee as a source of ideas seems to be indicated.

The interviews conducted for this book revealed that the workers themselves are virtually untapped resources for ideas. In other words, cities are underutilizing the intellectual capacities of their public employees. If civil servants were allowed more flexibility in the design of workshifts, administrative tasks, and job descriptions, they might well make a much-needed contribution to the welfare of the personnel community.

The future of the urban personnel community depends, however, on how well the participants—that is to say, the interest groups—can orchestrate their performances, for it is the interest groups that can either generate discord or achieve harmony. To paraphrase *Hamlet,* like the urban personnel drama itself, such groups can be the thing wherein to catch the conscience of the king.

NOTES

1: INTRODUCTION

1. Alexander George, "Political Leadership and Social Change in American Cities," *Daedalus* (Fall 1968), p. 1197.
2. Jeffrey Pressman, "Preconditions of Mayoral Leadership," *American Political Science Review,* vol. 66, no. 2 (June 1972), p. 512.
3. Jeffrey M. Berry, *Lobbying for the People* (Princeton: Princeton University Press, 1977), p. 7.
4. *Griggs* v. *Duke Power Company,* 401 U.S. 424 (1971).
5. *McCarty* v. *Philadelphia Civil Service Commission,* 96 S.Ct. 1155 (1976).
6. David Bird, "Residency Law for City Employees," *New York Times* (Dec. 12, 1978), p. B1.
7. *Abood* v. *Detroit Board of Education,* 431 U.S. 209 (1977).
8. E. E. Schattschneider, *Party Government* (New York: Rinehart, 1942), p. 51.
9. Karl Mannheim, *Ideology and Utopia* (New York: Harvest Book, 1936), p. 203.

2: GENTEEL REFORMERS AND THE POLITICAL MACHINE

1. Sidney I. Pomerantz, *New York: An American City 1783-1803: A Study of Urban Life* (Port Washington, N.Y.: Ira J. Friedman, 1965), p. 62-63.
2. Ibid., p. 503; for a discussion of colonial cities see Richard Wade, *The Urban Frontier* (Cambridge, Mass: Harvard University Press, 1959); Carl Bridenbaugh, *Cities in Revolt* (New York: Alfred Knopf, 1955); and Charles N. Glaab, *The American City* (Homewood, Ill.: Dorsey Press, 1963).
3. Ibid., p. 51.
4. Ira Rosenwaike, *Population History of New York City* (Syracuse: Syracuse University Press, 1972), p. 16.
5. William O. Winter, *The Urban Policy* (New York: Dodd, Mead, 1969), pp. 232-233.
6. The source of this historical material is Edward Robb Ellis, *The Epic of New York* (New York: Coward-McCann, 1966).

7.   For a discussion of early New York City volunteer firemen, see Lowell M. Limpus, *History of the New York Fire Department* (New York: E. P. Dutton, 1940); also see Richard Calhoun, "New York City Fire Department Reorganization 1865–1870: A Civil War Legacy," *New-York Historical Society Quarterly,* vol. 60, (January/April 1976), pp. 1–34.

8.   For an excellent description of the impact of population on the city's rapid growth, see Harold C. Syrett, *The City of Brooklyn 1865-1898* (New York: Columbia University Press, 1944); also see Ellis, op. cit.

9.   For a discussion of the early New York aristocracy, see Gabriel Almond, "Plutocracy and Politics in New York City," (Ph.D. dissertation, University of Chicago, 1939); Dixon Ryan Fox, *The Decline of Aristocracy in the Politics of New York* (New York: Columbia University Press, 1919); Edward Passen, *Riches Class and Power Before the Civil War* (Lexington, Mass: D. C. Heath, 1973); and also see Daniel Van Pelt, *Leslie's History of Greater New York* (New York: Arkell Publishing Co., 1898).

10.   See Arthur W. Macmahon, *The Statuary Sources of New York City Government* (New York: Columbia University Press, 1923), pp. 7–8.

11.   Seymour J. Mandelbaum, *Boss Tweed's New York* (New York: John Wiley, 1965), p. 5.

12.   Ibid.

13.   Leo Hershkowitz, *Tweed's New York* (Garden City, N.Y.: Anchor Press, 1977), p. xvi.

14.   William L. Riordan, *Plunkett of Tammany Hall* (New York: E. P. Dutton, 1963), pp. 12–13.

15.   Most of the literature on Tammany was written by reformers and journalists who sympathized with the reformer cause. See Edwin L. Godkin, "Criminal Politics," *North American Review,* vol. 150 (June 1890), pp. 706–723; John P. Bocock, "The Irish Conquest of Our Cities," *Nation,* vol. 17 (April 1894), pp. 185–195; Gustavus Meyers, *The History of Tammany Hall* (New York: published by the author, 1901); Harold Zink, *City Bosses in the United States: A Study of Twenty Municipal Bosses* (Durham, N.C.: Duke University Press, 1930); William J. Hartman, "Politics and Patronage" (New York: Ph.D. dissertation, Columbia University, 1952); Alexander B. Callow, *The Tweed Ring* (New York: Oxford University Press, 1966); and Lothrop Stoddard, *Master of Manhattan: The Life of Richrd Croker* (New York: Longmans, Green, 1939).

16.   Abby H. Ware and Abby G. Baker, *Municipal Government of the City of New York* (New York: Ginn, 1906), p. 35.

17.   Dorman Eaton, "Political Assessments," *Civil Service Record* (June 1882), p. 2.

18.   For a discussion of this point, see Francis Parkman, "The Failure of Universal Suffrage," *North American Review,* vol. 127 (July-August 1878), pp. 3–13; Richard Hofstadter, *The Age of Reform* (New York: Vintage Books, 1955); Gerald McFarland, *Mugwumps, Morals and Politics 1884-1920* (Amherst: University of Massachusetts, 1975); and also Dwight Waldo, *The Administrative State* (New York: Ronald Press, 1948).

19.   Richard Hofstadter, *Social Darwinism in American Thought* (Philadelphia: University of Pennsylvania Press, 1945).

20.   Everett Wheeler, "Civil Service Reform, American and Practical," *Civil Service Record,* vol. 1, no. 10 (March 1882), p. 26.

21.   Hofstadter, op. cit.

22.   Edwin L. Godkin, *The Danger of an Officeholding Aristocracy* (New York: G. P. Putnam's Sons, 1882), pp. 9–10.

23.   "The Church Congress," *Civil Service Record* (October 22, 1881), p. 5.

24.   Ibid.

25.   Henry Lambert, "Civil Service Reform and the Working Classes," *Civil Service Record,* vol. 11, no. 4 (September 1882), p. 31.

26. "Civic Reform in Municipal Government," *Civil Service Record* (April 1883), p. 85.

27. "Civil Service reform in State and City," *Civil Service Record* (February 1883), p. 70.

28. Lucius Wilmerding, Jr., *Government by Merit* (New York: McGraw-Hill, 1935), p. 126.

29. James Q. Wilson, "The Economy of Patronage," *Journal of Political Economy*, vol. 59, no. 4 (August 1961), p. 370.

30. *Civil Service Record* (November 1882), pp. 47–48.

31. William E. Mosher and J. Donald Kingley, *Public Personnel Administration* (New York: Harper, 1941).

32. Ibid.

33. Harry Kranz, "Are Merit and Equity Compatible," *Public Administration Review*, vol. 34, no. 5 (September/October 1974), p. 436.

34. Carl Fish, *Civil Service and Patronage* (Cambridge: Harvard University Press, 1920).

35. Ibid., p. 216.

36. Ari Hoogenboom, *Outlawing the Spoils* (Urbana: University of Illinois Press, 1961).

37. See Everett Wheeler, *Sixty Years of American Life* (New York: E. P. Dutton, 1917).

38. "Civil Service Reform in State and City," *Civil Service Record* (February 1882), p. 70.

39. Alfred Connable and Edward Silverfarb, *Tigers of Tammany: Nine Men Who Ran New York* (New York: Holt, Rinehart and Winston, 1967).

40. George E. Waring, *Street Cleaning: The Effect Upon Public Health, Public Morals and Municipal Prosperity* (New York: Doubleday and McClure, 1897), p. 21.

41. Henry Steele Commager, *The American Mind,* chapter 2.

42. Edward Robb Ellis, *The Epic of New York* (New York: Coward-McCann, 1966), p. 453.

43. George di L. Elcaness, *History of the Municipal Civil Service in New York City* (master's thesis, New York University, 1937), p. 95.

44. Lincoln Steffens, *The Shame of the Cities* (New York: Sagamore Press, 1957).

3: ACADEMIC REFORMERS AND THE POLITICS OF MAYORALTY CONTROL

1. Louis H. Pink, *Gaynor: The Tammany Man Who Swallowed the Tiger* (New York: International Press, 1931), p. 155.

2. Robert Moses, *The Civil Service of Great Britain* (New York: Columbia University, 1914).

3. Ibid.

4. Woodrow Wilson, "The Study of Administration," *Political Science Quarterly*, (June 1887); reprinted in Louis C. Gawthrop, *The Administrative Process and Democratic Theory* (Boston: Houghton Mifflin, 1970).

5. Frank Goodnow, *Politics and Administration: A Study in Government* (New York: Russell and Russell, 1900).

6. Cited in Samuel Haber, *Efficiency and Uplift* (Chicago: University of Chicago Press, 1964), p. 1.

7. Frederick W. Taylor, *The Principles of Scientific Management* (New York: Harper, 1911).

8. John Mitchel, "Efficiency and the Government," *Independent*, vol. 80 (November, 1914); see also "What We Have Done to New York" (May 10, 1915), pp. 237–239.

9. Charles Beard, "Appreciation," *Survey*, vol. 40 (July 13, 1918), pp. 332–333.

10.   This account relies on Haber, op. cit., chapter 2.

11.   Robert Caro, *The Power Broker: Robert Moses and the Fall of New York* (New York: Alfred Knopf, 1974), p. 77.

12.   *Report on Investigation of the Municipal Civil Service Commission and the Administration of the Civil Service and Rules Transmitted to the Legislature Feb. 1, 1915,* p. 62.

13.   See Arthur Mann, *LaGuardia Comes to Power* (New York: J. B. Lippincott, 1965).

14.   William Brown, "The Political and Administrative Leadership of Fiorello LaGuardia" (New York: Ph.D. dissertation, New York University, 1960), p. 98.

15.   Charles Belous, *Faith in Fusion* (New York: Vantage Press, 1951).

16.   Brown, op. cit., p. 318.

17.   Ibid., p. 334.

18.   Rexford Tugwell, *The Art of Politics* (Garden City, N.Y.: Doubleday, 1958), p. 102.

19.   For a discussion, see Demetrios Caraley, *New York City Deputy Mayor/ City Administrator* (New York: Citizen Budget Commission, 1966).

20.   Wallace Sayre and Herbert Kaufman, "Personnel Administration in Government of New York City," a report prepared for the Mayor's Committee on Management Survey of the City of New York, March, 1952. (Mimeographed).

21.   *Report to Mayor of City of New York and to State Civil Service Commission* (New York: Municipal Civil Service, January 1, 1952–December 31, 1952), p. 13.

22.   *A More Efficient and Responsive Municipal Government: Final Report to the Legislature of the State Charter Revision Commission for New York City* (New York: State Charter Revision Commission, March 31, 1977), p. 29.

23.   Ibid.

24.   Wilbur C. Rich, "Conflicts and Status Inequities in Public Organizations: A Cause for Low Productivity?" unpublished manuscript.

25.   E. S. Savas and Sigmund G. Ginsburg, "The Civil Service: A Meritless System?" *Public Interest,* no. 32 (Summer 1973), pp. 70–85.

26.   Impression of remarks by State Senator Roy Goodman at Forum of New York City Bar Association, Summer 1975.

27.   Leslie Maitland, "Koch's Plan Strengthens Disciplining of Workers," *New York Times* (May 21, 1978), p. B1.

28.   Murray Edelman, *The Symbolic Uses of Politics* (Urbana: University of Illinois Press, 1967), pp. 44–45.

29.   Ibid., p. 47.

30.   David Bird, "Residency Law for City Employees," *New York Times* (December 12, 1978), p. B1.

31.   Ibid., p. B1.

32.   The ruling was upheld in the Court of Appeals; see Ronald Smothers, "Residency Rules Overturned for City Uniform Forces," *New York Times* (April 30, 1980), p. B1.

33.   Wilbur C. Rich, "Civil Servants, Municipalities, and Courts," *Public Administration Review,* vol. 37 (September-October 1977), p. 518.

34.   E. J. Dionne "Koch is Upset as Governor Signs a 2-Year Extension of Heart Bill," *New York Times* (June 30, 1979), p. 23.

35.   "Critique of the Plan for a Management Service for the City of New York," *Citizens Union of the City of New York* (1979), p. 10 (mimeographed).

4: UNIONS AS INTEREST GROUPS IN PERSONNEL POLICY

1.   Lothrop Stoddard, *Master of Manhattan: The Life of Richard Croker* (New York: Longmans, Green, 1939), p. 41.

2.   Edward M. Shepard, *The Competitive Test and Civil Service of State and Cities* (New York: Society of Political Education, 1884), p. 39.

3.   Clifford W. Patton, *The Battle for Municipal Reform* (Washington, D.C.: American Council on Public Affairs, 1940), p. 12.

4.   Wirt Howe, *New York at the Turn of the Century 1899-1916* (Toronto: privately printed, 1946), p. 68.

5.   See Emma Schweppe, *The Firemen's and Patrolmen's Unions in the City of New York* (New York: King Crown Press, 1948); and also David Zuskind, *One Thousand Strikes of Government Employees* (New York: Columbia University Press, 1940).

6.   See *The Police Problem in New York City* (New York: Bureau of City Betterment, November 1906).

7.   Sterling D. Spero, *Government as Employer* (New York: Rensen Press, 1948), p. 211.

8.   Ralph Jones, "City Employee Unions in New York and Chicago,"(Ph.D. dissertation, Harvard University, 1972), chapter 4.

9.   Richard N. Billing and John Greenspan, *Power to the Public Worker* (New York: Robert B. Luce, 1974).

10.   Jones, op. cit., pp. 122–24.

11.   Sterling Spero, "Have Public Employees the Right to Strike—Maybe," *National Municipal Review,* vol. 30 (September 1941), pp. 524–528; Eliot Kaplan, "Have Public Employees the Right to Strike—No," *National Municipal Review,* vol. 30 (September 1941), pp. 518–523; Arthur W. Macmahon, "The New York City Transit System: Public Ownership, Civil Service and Collective Bargaining," *Political Science Quarterly* (June 1941), pp. 161–98.

12.   See Harry H. Wellington and Ralph K. Winter, Jr., *The Unions and Cities* (Washington, D. C., Brookings Institution, 1971); David T. Stanley and Carole L. Cooper, *Managing Local Government under Pressure* (Washington, D.C.: Brookings Institution, 1972).

13.   Data supplied by New York City's Office of Collective Bargaining.

14.   Raymond Horton, *Municipal Labor Relations; Lessons of Lindsay-Wagner Years* (New York: Praeger, 1973), pp. 35–36.

15.   Approved December 1971 by the City Council, *Local Laws of the City of New York,* no. 1 (1972), City Record.

16.   Horton, op. cit., p. 120.

17.   David Lewin, "Collective Bargaining and the Right to Strike" in Lawrence Chickering, ed., *Public Employee Unions* (San Francisco: Institute for Contemporary Studies, 1976), p. 153.

18.   Edward N. Costikyan, "Who Runs the City Government?" *New York Post* (May 1969), p. 45.

19.   Konrad Lorenz, *On Aggression* (New York: Harcourt Brace, 1974).

20.   Sayre and Kaufman, op. cit., pp. 419–420.

21.   Truman, op. cit.

22.   Mancur Olson, *The Logic of Collective Action* (Cambridge: Harvard University Press, 1965), p. 136.

5: THE NEW FISCAL MANAGERS AND THE PERSONNEL ARENA

1.   "Briefing," *Fiscal Observer,* vol. 11, nos. 12 and 13 (June 15, 1978), p. 1.

2.   Ibid., p. 2.

3.   "A Summary of Remarks by Herbert Bienstock before the New York Senate Standing Committee on Labor" (March 9, 1976), p. 3 (mimeographed).

4.   For another view, see Herbert Bienstock, "More People Work in New York City than in 44 of 50 States," and "Educational Developments Viewed as Highly Favorable in Years Ahead," *Bureau of Labor Statistics, Middle Atlantic Region,* U.S. Department of Labor news release (March 4, 1976), p. 1.

5.   See "The Fortune Directories of the 500 Largest Industrial Corporations," *Fortune* (May 1971), pp. 170–204.

6. Eli Ginzberg et al., *Corporate Headquarter Complex in New York City* (New York: Conservation of Human Resources, 1978), pp. 37–54.

7. Congressional Budget Office, *New York City Fiscal Problem: Its Origins, Potential Repercussions, and Some Alternative Policy Responses* (Washington, D.C., Congress Budget Office, 1975).

8. Ibid., p. 9.

9. Ibid.

10. Cited in *Fiscal Observer*, vol. 11, no. 9 (May 4, 1978), p. 1.

11. Ibid., p. 2.

12. Jack Newfield and Paul DuBrul, *The Abuse of Power* (New York: Penguin Books, 1978), p. 182.

13. "City Layoffs: The Effects on Minorities and Women," *New York City Commission on Human Rights* (April 1976), pp. 7–8.

14. Ibid., p. 11.

15. "Five Funds Sell MAC Bonds Turning a Profit," *New York Times* (July 25, 1979) p. B6; see also Anna Quindlen, "Five Pension Funds began Selling MAC Bonds," *New York Times* (July 24, 1979), p. A1.

16. James Norman, "Koch: I am so mad at MAC," *New York Post* (March 5, 1979), p. 7.

17. Ibid.

18. Ibid.

19. Lee Dembart, "Lazard, Stung by Koch, Ends MAC Role," *New York Times* (March 8, 1979), p. 1.

20. Fred Ferretti, *The Year the Big Apple Went Bust* (New York: G. P. Putnam, 1976), pp. 415–416.

21. Newfield and DuBrul, op. cit., p. 340.

22. Interview with a fiscal manager.

6: PERSONNEL POLICY AS A REFLECTION OF GROUP INTEREST

1. Wallace Sayre and Herbert Kaufman, *Governing New York City* (New York: W. W. Norton, 1960), p. 366.

2. Ibid., p. 370.

3. Civil Service Assembly, Position-Classification in the Public Service (Chicago: Civil Service Assembly, 1942), p. 3.

4. Ibid., p. 56.

5. O. Glenn Stahl, *Public Personnel Administration* (New York: Harper and Row, 1976), p. 75.

6. Phillip Schrag, *Counsel to the Deceived* (New York: Pantheon, 1972), p. 30.

7. Ibid., p. 33.

8. Ibid., p. 34.

9. Ibid., p. 34.

10. See *Personnel Reforms for New York City* (New York State Charter Revision, January 1975).

11. Everett Wheeler, *Sixty Years of American Life*, p. 304.

12. Wallace Sayre, "The Triumph of Technique over Purpose," *Public Administration Review*, vol. 8 (Spring 1948).

13. Wallace Sayre and Herbert Kaufman, *Personnel Administration in Government,* (March 1954).

14. Lester G. Seligman, *Patterns of Recruitment* (Chicago: Rand McNally, 1974), p. 14.

15. Albert Glickman et al., *Top Management Development and Succession* (New York: Macmillan, 1968), p. 32.

16. Melville Dalton, *Men Who Manage* (New York: John Wiley, 1959), p. 58.

17. David Roger, *The Management of Big Cities* (Beverly Hills, Calif.: Sage Publications, 1971), p. 37.

18. The data for this study were based on the results from a questionnaire sent to 226 persons identified as members of the city Managerial Pay Plan. The new pay plan was initiated by then mayor, John V. Lindsay, as a reform measure to encourage better recruitment and retention of agency managers. The plan covers a variety of individuals ranging from manager of a city hospital laundry to deputy administrator of one of the largest city agencies. To supplement the questionnaires, more than a hundred face-to-face interviews were conducted with officials at all levels of city government and are cited in the text as interviews with civil servants. Anonymity was usually a precondition for granting interviews. I have honored these requests.

19. Interview with a civil servant.

20. Kenneth Prewitt, *The Recruitment of Political Leaders: A Study of Citizen-Politicians* (Indianapolis: Bobbs-Merrill, 1970), chapter 1.

21. Interview with a civil servant.

22. "Classification and Compensation of Career and Salary Plan Positions," Rule XI, *Rules and Regulations of the City Personnel Director,* (Department of Personnel, The City of New York, 1978), p. 32.

23. "Uniformed Services in 10 Leading Cities," *The New York Times* (October 14, 1976), p. 42.

24. N.Y. (Civil Service Law), SS 75–76 (McKinney).

7: SUMMARY AND RECOMMENDATIONS

1. Theodore J. Lowi, *At the Pleasure of the Mayor* (New York: Free Press of Glencoe, 1964).

2. Murray Edelman, *The Symbolic Uses of Politics* (Urbana: University of Illinois Press, 1964), p. 31.

3. Ferdinand Mount, *The Theatre of Politics* (New York: Schocken Books, 1973), p. 233.

4. H. H. Gerth and C. Wright Mills, *From Max Weber* (New York: Oxford University Press, 1946), p. 18.

5. E. E. Schattschneider, *Party Government* (New York: Rinehart, 1942).

6. 96 S. Ct. 2673 (1976).

7. Michael Lipsky, "Protest as Political Resource," *American Political Science Review,* vol. 72 (December 1968), pp. 211–219.

8. Interview with a civil service manager.

9. Wallace Sayre and Herbert Kaufman, *Governing New York City* (New York: W. W. Norton, 1965), p. 738.

10. Douglas McGregor, "An Uneasy Look at Performance Appraisal," *Harvard Business Review* (May/June 1957), p. 94.

11. Lee Dembart, "State Finds City's Raises Not Met by Productivity," *New York Times* (December 17, 1978), p. 64.

INDEX